THE ELEMENTS
OF AUDIENCE ANALYSIS

THE ELEMENTS OF AUDIENCE ANALYSIS

Jan Youga
GORDON COLLEGE

MACMILLAN PUBLISHING COMPANY
New York

Collier Macmillan Publishers
London

Macmillan Publishing Company
866 Third Avenue, New York, New York 10022

Collier Macmillan Canada, Inc.

Library of Congress Cataloging-in-Publication Data

Youga, Janet Martha.
    The elements of audience analysis / Jan Youga.
        p.   cm.
    Includes index.
    ISBN 0-02-431050-6
    1. Public speaking.   I. Title.
PN4121.Y58 1989
808.5'–dc19   88-11788
                                                                 CIP

Printing: 1 2 3 4 5 6 7   Year: 9 0 1 2 3 4 5

To Jim—
Who taught me to unclench my fists

Preface

In the fourth century B.C., Plato reminded his pupil Phaedrus that he must understand the nature of his audience if he hoped to be a successful speaker, and that he must

> . . . discover the kind of speech that matches each type of nature. When that is accomplished, he must arrange and adorn each speech in such a way as to present complicated and unstable souls with complex speeches, speeches exactly attuned to every changing mood of the complicated soul—while the simple soul must be presented with simple speech. (*Phaedrus*, 277, trans. Hembold and Rabinowitz)

Since that time, speakers and writers have grappled with the idea that when they write, they write for someone, and that if they want that someone to listen and understand, they must take that reader's needs into account as they write. Whether the writer actually knows the reader or must try to imagine or "invoke" an audience, to use Ede and Lunsford's term, the reader is an ever-present part of the composing process—as significant as the person doing the writing, the message being conveyed, and the reason behind the writing. As James Britton points out, each act of writing always involves two fundamental questions: "What is the writing for?" and "Who is it for?"

An awareness and understanding of audience has the power to make a significant difference in the quality of prose we produce. It makes us realize that we do not write just to fill up pages or to complete an assignment, but to communicate something to people in a way that will really make them want to listen. A sense of audience can make us aware of the power, versatility, and consequences of effective writing.

The book begins, in fact, with a discussion and demonstration of how audience can affect writing. It then moves on in Chapter 2 to a discussion of how audience influences style. Chapters 3 through 6 are designed to help writers imagine their readers and to anticipate how their message will be received by various audiences. The book ends with an examination of the whole writing process and of how an awareness of audience influences every decision a writer makes while producing a paper. I have tried to provide numerous brief examples which are meant to serve, not as models necessarily, but as the basis for a discussion of the principles and ideas raised in the book.

I have tried to share this information on audience in the same way that I share it with my students, that is, as something that all writers, myself included, need in order to write effectively. Therefore, I have not approached the subject as if I were imposing rules on others' writing. There are no imperatives, no "Ten Commandments for Audience Analysis," no "Rigid Rules for Writing to Readers." Rather, I have tried to explain the concept and its consequences for writing in a way that will help *guide* the process of audience analysis.

I would like to thank the following individuals who reviewed the book: Russel K. Durst, University of Cincinnati; Leonard G. Heidreth, Northern Michigan University; Francis Hubbard, Marquette University; Thomas Pearsall, University of Minnesota; Sally Sullivan, University of North Carolina; and R. J. Wiley, University of Arizona.

I would also like to thank all of my students who have gone through the process of learning about audience with me, especially Toni Minehart, who held down the fort while I was revising, and "the boys" — Mark, Scott, Bruce, and Tim — because they care about teaching. Thanks also goes to the students whose work provided samples for this book, especially to Brian Junghans and Michelle Sturgeon, and to Don Clemons

and Cherie Rudolph who provided the extended examples in
Chapters 2 and 8. I thank Cleo Martin at the University of
Iowa who first made me aware of the importance of teaching
audience when she said, "Why don't you have your students
write to seventh graders?" And thanks to Betty McMahan
who gave me the chance to do this book. I am also grateful
to my editor, Tony English, and to the reviewers for their
helpful comments. Finally, thanks to Jim — for everything.

Jan Youga

Contents

PART ONE

Writing for an Audience

Closed 9:30–1:00 tomorrow
for the funeral

Captured in this little sign posted on the door of a cafe in a small Minnesota town is the essence of the concept "audience." When I saw this sign, enough information was communicated to me so that I knew I could not get a late breakfast or early lunch the next day. But I also knew the sign would say much more to the people who lived in that community. They all, no doubt, knew who had died and under what circumstances and why this death meant that the cafe had to close down completely for three and a half hours on a business day. In fact, they would probably all be attending "the funeral" themselves. For me, all this information remained a mystery.

The reason for the mystery was simple—I was not the intended audience for the message written on that sign. I was an outsider just passing through the town (a rare occurrence for this place), so my need for a more thorough explanation was not anticipated. The sign was written for the cafe's "regulars" who found it perfectly comprehensible because it was written for them. They were the *audience* for the message.

Audience can be defined as the intended receiver of the writer's message. To this intended receiver, the message is usually perfectly clear. The audience has a context for the writing and a purpose for reading it. The writer has also taken the audience's needs into account by providing background information when it is needed. The cryptic sign on the door was meaningful for the intended receivers because they understood the context of the funeral and how it related to the restaurant; and since the writer knew the readers would have this context, no more information was necessary.

On the other hand, readers other than the intended receivers may understand the message's words and even some of its significance, but much of its real meaning will likely be lost. Although I understand what a funeral is, "the funeral" did not have the special meaning to me that it did to the townspeople. I understood the message in general terms, but did not have the complete understanding that the intended readers had.

This explanation makes the concept of audience seem perfectly simple, but most writers find it a very difficult idea to incorporate into their writing. When the concept is explained to us, we can all nod in agreement at this commonsense notion. But to really understand what audience is and how it affects a piece of writing, we need to look at it more closely in terms of the rhetorical situation involved in communicating.

Chapter 1

Audience and the Rhetorical Situation

In any given writing situation, three elements will always be present to form what is called the communications triangle: the writer, the audience, and the subject. These in turn lead to the three major purposes for writing:

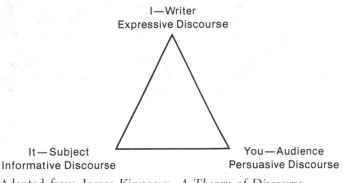

I—Writer
Expressive Discourse

It—Subject
Informative Discourse

You—Audience
Persuasive Discourse

Adapted from James Kinneavy, A *Theory of Discourse*

All three elements are present in any piece of writing—someone is always writing to someone about something. But it is the effort to touch someone with our words, to reach an audience, that really creates the dynamic interaction at work in genuine communication.

Audience and the Writer

Dear Mom,
   You know that money you said I could have if I went over my budget this month? Well, I'm over. Send cash—quick!

When we put pen to paper, it is generally with the assumption that someone is going to read what we write. Although sometimes we write only for ourselves, we usually are trying to communicate with someone else when we write. Sometimes our relationship to our audience is very clear and very specific, as in the above letter to Mom. Other times, we only have a vague and general idea of who our readers are, as when we write an essay for a scholarship board.

What should be obvious, however, is that we do not ask Mom and the board for money in the same way. With Mom we can be very direct and very informal; we know we are loved and the funds will probably follow soon. But a quick note dashed off to the board will leave the board members quite unimpressed. With this audience, we need to prove that we deserve the money first and then request it in a formal, polite way.

In other words, our relationship with our chosen audience helps us to select the proper tone of voice and the amount and kind of information we need to provide for our readers. This means that before we write, we must be clear about who our readers are and what our relationship to them is.

Audience and the Subject

Did you get that stuff done today?

For most readers, the above sentence would communicate very little. We would have no idea what "stuff" needed to be done. If we found such a note, we would know immediately that it was intended for someone else (or that we had fallen asleep during an important conversation). On the other hand, if this were a note written to us by one of our roommates about some "stuff" that had been clearly defined in a conversation the night before, the message would be perfectly clear. If we were the intended audience, the information in the sentence would serve as a sufficient reminder of what needed to be done. If we were not, the note would lack necessary details.

How much information we need to provide for an audience, then, depends on our relationship to our readers. A message between two close friends will need very little background; references such as "stuff" need not be defined. But most writing is done for people who do not understand what we say as well as our close friends do, and we need to provide much more information for them. A history teacher, for example, would not be satisfied with an exam answer that simply stated that the student had learned "a lot of stuff about the Civil War."

Audience and Purpose

Writings of a political candidate:

Letter to Family: In every speech, I keep talking about what horrible blunders the Governor has made, but I can't help wondering what terrible mistakes my opponent four years from now will have to hold against me if I win this election.

Speech to Voters: The current administration has made mistake after mistake and spent all of its time trying to cover up those mistakes. Consequently, nothing's been done about them. This administration is proving itself incompetent. A vote for me is a vote for competence and integrity.

Memo to Election Committee: Outlined below is the plan for the next meeting (on our opponent's mistakes), which will take place at 3:00 on February 2 in the conference room.

The three excerpts above show how the same speaker (a political candidate) could approach the same subject (an opponent's mistakes) differently, depending on the purpose and audience for the writing.

In the letter to family members, the focus is on the candidate's feelings about the election and worries about the future. The writing is *expressive*, revealing personal thoughts. The family does not need to be persuaded of the candidate's worth; if so, the worries of this letter would probably not be shared. The writers, although providing members of the family with some information, is not writing to tell them what would be considered the "news" of the campaign. The purpose is a personal one, meant to share feelings and fears with close fan.ily members.

In the speech to voters, the focus is on producing, by any means available, the desired voting behavior in the audience. The speaker sounds confident in accusing the current administration of misconduct. The personal revelation of insecurity is completely gone. There is also no attempt to provide objective information or specific support for the accusations. In other words, the purpose is to be *persuasive*.

The memo, on the other hand, does not need to be persuasive; the staff is already on the candidate's side. It also does not need to be expressive since the speaker wants to focus on the meeting and not on personal feelings about it. The message simply needs to be *informative* so the staff knows the plan for the next meeting. The focus is on the information itself.

These three excerpts illustrate the three major purposes we have in writing:

1. *expressive*, which focuses on writing for self or on sharing a part of ourselves or our experiences with someone else;
2. *persuasive*, which focuses on producing some change in our audience's attitudes or behavior; and
3. *informative*, which focuses on communicating or explaining a specific subject matter to our audience.

Three in One

Before examining each of these purposes more closely, I would like to emphasize that they are not always separate and distinct in each piece of writing. A persuasive essay must contain information. An expressive piece may be very moving. The information contained in a particular book may persuade someone to take action. And some pieces of writing may contain all three purposes. For example, the Declaration of Independence is often cited as a document that has mixed purposes. In its strong statement of beliefs, its use of first person pronouns, and its idiosyncratic punctuation, it is very expressive, almost like a creed ("—We hold these truths to be self-evident . . . "). However, its list of grievances is very informative, as is its declaration of independence. But of course the document is also meant to be persuasive, to convince others that this declaration is justified and well within the rights of the people involved.

In other words, these three purposes overlap and are often found to varying degrees in the same piece of writing. The categories are not meant to be rigid. Still, the terms are useful in identifying the major purpose the writer is trying to achieve and the major effect the writing is supposed to have on the audience.

Audience in Expressive Writing

It's snowing, snowing, snowing. La, la, la, la, la, la, la, la, la. It's snowing. Yeah!

These expressions of delight were written in the journal of a foreign student after her first experience with snow. The excerpt illustrates one of the major audiences for expressive writing — *ourselves*. Writings contained in diaries or journals are usually expressive. They are personal records of events or feelings that are important only to us — as the snowfall is important to the writer of the journal.

Writers also often write expressively when they use journals or brainstorming lists as prewriting and when they work out the first drafts of their papers. The technique serves as a way to get started, to get many ideas down on paper before the more methodical work of organizing begins.

Expressive writing also includes letters to friends and family.

Although these letters may contain much news, that information is only interesting to the audience because it is news about us. We are still the focus of the piece. In the same way, autobiographies are also a form of expressive discourse because they are personal accounts of the writer's life and interesting to readers only because of who the writer is.

Finally, we write expressively to people who may not yet know or be close to us, but who are nevertheless receptive to what we have to say. Classmates are a good example of this audience, and the narratives written to help classmates get acquainted are good examples of this kind of expressive discourse.

Because expressive writing, then, focuses on self and is written to ourselves or a close or receptive audience, a personal voice and subject matter are appropriate.

Audience in Persuasive Writing

"Let's go to see a movie tonight."

The relationship between the writer and the audience in persuasive writing is very complicated. First, persuasive writing may be aimed at someone who agrees with us. The response to the movie suggestion may be, "Yeah, let's." Or the persuasion may be aimed at someone who somewhat agrees with us but wants certain modifications to be made: "Good idea, but let's go tomorrow instead." Or we may meet serious opposition: "I hate going to movies. You know that. Why do you keep bringing that up? Go yourself if you want to go, and leave me alone."

Persuasion is further complicated by what we want from our listeners. The speaker may want the audience to act in a specific way as in the first statement about the movie; the speaker wants the audience to go to a movie tonight. But perhaps the speaker only wants general confirmation of an attitude: "Would you be willing to go to a movie sometime?" or even, "Do you like movies?" Finally, the speaker may want no present or future action at all but a change in the person's attitude about movies in general: "I know you hate movies. But I don't understand why. I love them, and you know that. I think you pretend to dislike them just to make me mad! Why can't you do something for me for a change?"

A final complication in persuasion concerns the subject matter. Usually, the writer cares about the topic, or there would be no desire to speak to someone else about it. In other words, when we write persuasively, we usually have some stake in the topic. The stake may be minor; the movie may just be "something to do," and a rejection of the idea will not matter much. But often the stake is large, as in the last response to the movie suggestion. Here the speaker equates the rejection of the movie with a rejection of self, and an ulterior motive (making the speaker angry) is attributed to the audience.

In other words, persuasion is difficult. And any piece of writing that is meant to persuade must take into account the attitude of the audience, the outcome that is expected from the audience, and the personal stake the writer has in that outcome.

Because persuasive writing, then, is focused on trying to produce some change in the audience, the subject matter is usually something which the writer cares about. But since it is written for readers who may range from being receptive to openly hostile, the voice used could also range from suggesting to demanding.

Audience in Informative Writing

au·di·ence / *n*   3a: a group of listeners or spectators

When the editors of *Webster's Ninth New Collegiate Dictionary* wrote this definition, their purpose was not to persuade us that the definition was right. They know that when we look up a word, we already assume that the dictionary will give us the right answer. They were also not trying to share with us any personal meaning the word has come to have in their lives. They would not eliminate a word because they did not like it or put an obscure definition first because they thought it was clever. Rather, the editors stick to their purpose of providing us with information about the current meaning of this word in the English language. This same focus on information can be found in many other forms of writing: news releases, weather reports, research papers, encyclopedias, annual reports, recipes, computer manuals, directions, and phone books.

The audience for all of these writings is someone looking for information. The audience is not usually critical—we do not really doubt that a number listed in the phone book will get us the party we want; in fact, we are surprised when it does not and often assume we made an error in dialing rather than that the book is wrong. Similarly, the audience is usually detached from the writing. We do not feel involved with an encyclopedia as we do with a letter from a good friend. At the same time, there is an assumption of honesty and integrity; we would not buy a map that we felt would misdirect us.

Because informative writing, then, focuses on the subject and is written for a detached audience, a formal, less personal voice and accurate information are expected.

Why Audience Matters

> Transportation is a major concern of people today. There are many forms of transportation available today. Cars, boats, buses, and planes are all examples of transportation.

There are many things wrong with these opening sentences of a student paper. But the most obvious fault is that no one would want to read them; in fact, only an English teacher being paid to teach this student would get past the first sentence and then only with great dread of what is likely to follow.

This student is following a typical bit of advice given in textbooks—begin with a general idea and move toward more specific, supporting statements. But there is a difference between a general idea and a generalization that contains no real idea at all. "Transportation is a major concern of people today" is meaningless. How many people do we know personally who would rank transportation among their major worries of the day? They very well might if their cars failed to start that morning and they needed a way to work; but generally, most "people today" would not make transportation a top priority on their worry list. In addition, those people who really are concerned about transportation—air traffic controllers, bus drivers, train conductors, truckers—know that most people do not care about transportation. In fact, they are all too aware that people take transportation for granted until something goes wrong.

In other words, the generalization is simply untrue both for people in general and for people concerned with transportation. But the writer, of course, is not aware of this because he is not thinking about a real reader's response to his ideas. This complete lack of audience awareness becomes even more obvious when we look at the entire paper (reprinted below) because the thesis of this paper is that 16-year-olds should not be given cars until they are ready to handle the responsibility. The real audience, then, should have been either 16-year-olds who want cars and need to be reminded of the responsibilities of owning a vehicle or parents who are considering giving cars to their 16-year-old children. Neither of these audiences could have even been anticipated from these opening lines.

If the writer, an 18-year-old college freshman who had found out the hard way about the responsibilities of owning a car, had selected one of these audiences, he would have known what his relationship was to his readers: what tone of voice to use in addressing them; what topics to focus on and emphasize; and what his purpose was. Without this knowledge, the student could only write a generic paper—one written by anyone, to anyone, about anything.

If we look at this transportation paper in more detail, we can see quite clearly why audience matters.

Student Paper
TEENAGE DRIVING

    Transportation is a major concern of people today. There are many forms of transportation

available today. Cars, boats, buses, and planes
are all examples of transportation. All of these
forms of transportation are acceptable, but, for
use by the home owner, a car is the only practical
form. The car is usually acquired when a person
turns sixteen years old. However, cars should
not be given to teens just because they turn
sixteen.

Turning sixteen means being able to drive
for most teenagers. Most teens say that having a
car makes them feel mature and gives them a sense
of responsibility. A car gives teens something
they have never had before, mobility. Teens say
that this mobility causes them to be more responsible. Having to chauffeur around the children
in the family, keep appointments, maintain the
car, as well as pay for the car, insurance, and
gas all help to make a person responsible. Teens
tend to believe that turning sixteen instantly
makes them responsible people. They also believe
that instantly their parents should think of them
as very responsible people. Responsibility comes
after teens prove themselves, not instantaneously.

Parents should realize that there are several disadvantages to giving teens a car right
when they turn sixteen. The sheer cost of a car
today makes it a disadvantage to own one. Since
teens go to school all day they may only work
part time, if at all. The down payment alone
would wipe out the savings of most teens. However, if a teen is able to get by the down payment and the monthly payment, he/she faces financial devastation in insurance payments. If the
teen has inherited some money along the way and
can get past these first obstacles, there is
still the problem of gas. Even if they can come
up with all the money they need somehow, they
will still face other responsibilities. Some
teens are just not ready for this.

Teens of today need cars more than any other
generation. However, they need to be responsible
enough to handle a car properly. Parents--keep
the teens of today alive. Do not let your children

drive unless you as a parent feel that they are
ready to face this responsibility.

Analysis

In the first paragraph, several possible audiences are identified: people today, people concerned with transportation,
home owners, 16-year-olds, and people who might give cars
to 16-year-olds. As we read further in the paper, though, it
becomes clear that only two of these are relevant. Paragraph
2 is addressed to 16-year-olds, and paragraphs 3 and 4 are
written to parents. To teens he wants to say, "It's not as easy
as it looks." And to parents his advice is, "You may not be
doing them a favor if you give them a car before they're
ready for the responsibility." Both of these ideas are valuable,
and a successful paper could be constructed around either
audience. But the student needs to make up his mind and
restructure the paper focusing on one audience only.

How could this be done? Assume the student decided to
do an essay for *Parents* magazine. The essay could then be
rewritten as the following example illustrates.

Revision with Clear Audience: Parents

WHEN YOUR TEEN WANTS A CAR

It's your child's sixteenth birthday and as
you watch your teenager being congratulated by
friends and family, you realize how grown-up your
child has become. And yet, how often do you still
have to nag your almost-adult family member to
mow the yard, take out the garbage, or clean up
that cluttered bedroom? Your teenager seems to
be an odd combination of mature adult and irre-
sponsible child.

Which is why you flinched when your teenager
asked for the inevitable sixteenth-birthday gift
--a car. On the one hand, it would be nice not
to have to play constant chauffeur for the end-
less basketball games, dances, movies, and school

activities. On the other hand, you know you'll
worry every time you hear that engine start.

How can you handle this situation?

The best advice is not to feel guilty if
you decide against buying the car. Many teenagers
simply are not ready for the responsibility. But
make sure you are being fair in your decision:

Can you cite specific instances in which
you have depended on your child and been disappointed?
Does your child have specific duties around
the house that are continually neglected?
Have you given your child enough opportunities to prove responsibility in meaningful ways?

If you decide to buy your teenager a car,
make sure to point out all the financial responsibilities that will go with it:

How will the car be financed? Is it an out-
right gift, or is it to be bought with a loan
your teenager must repay?
Who will pay for gas, insurance, maintenance, and repairs?

Also, make sure that your teenager understands that the car will mean new family responsibilities and not just new freedom:

How often will your teenager be available
to serve as chauffeur for other family members?
How often will your teenager be available
to run errands?
Is your teenager ready to make and keep
appointments with dentists, doctors, and employ-
ers without reminders from you?
Is your teenager ready to make time for
maintenance and repairs, or will you be expected
to "take the car in"?

Finally, it is most important that you talk
to your teenager about any decision you make. If
you decide against the car, be sure your child
knows why. If you buy the car, make certain the
responsibilities that go with the car are clear,

as well as the consequences of not fulfilling
those duties.

These bits of advice will probably still
not stop your heart from pounding when you hear
the engine start on a Friday night, but they may
give you some confidence that you tried to make
your decision wisely and with the welfare of your
teenager in mind.

Analysis

Selecting a specific audience (parents) clarifies the information the writer was trying to communicate (that parents should
consider the decision of buying a car very carefully) and the
purpose of the message (to offer some advice, a mild form
of persuasion, and to provide some information about how
to go about taking this advice). The paper is no longer vague
and general. It has a clear and specific voice, subject matter,
and purpose *because* it has a clear audience.

Revision with Clear Audience: 16-Year-Olds

On the other hand, if the student had decided to write to
teenagers in his former high school through the school newspaper, the essay might have been written like this:

SO YOU WANT TO GET A CAR

You can picture yourself now, cruising down
Main Street and around the school parking lot--
the envy of all your friends. If you think about
it long enough, you can even feel the keys to
your new car in your hand.

And it wouldn't be just for fun. You need a
car to get to work, to basketball, to the mall,
and you definitely need it for dates. Your parents complain every time they have to drive you
anywhere. You'd be doing them a big favor if you
had your own wheels.

But before you start nagging them about it,
let me tell you a few things I found out when I
got my first car.

It costs money--lots of it. First there's
the cost of the car or the payments every month.
And then there's the additional cost of gas,
maintenance, and insurance. If you manage to pay
the deductible after your first fender-bender,
wait until you see how your premium will go up.
Unless you recently received a large inheritance
or your parents are very generous, you'd better
plan on quitting school and getting a full-time
job so you can support this new vehicle.

It's also a lot of responsibility. Once you
get a car, it's true you won't have to be chauf-
feured around; instead, you will be the one doing
the driving. Suddenly, every time your sisters
and brothers need to go somewhere, yours will be
the only car that's available.

Finally, there's the problem with friends.
Not only will they want a chauffeur, too, but
they may pressure you in other ways. They may
want to go "joy riding" or to use your car as a
safe place to drink. It's hard to say no when
they're telling you how wonderful your new car
is.

It's natural to want a car at 16, and you
probably feel you're ready for the responsibility. Maybe you are. But you need to be sure before
those imaginary keys become real.

Analysis

Once again, selecting an audience clarifies the information
the writer needs to include (the costs, responsibilities, and
dangers of car ownership) and the purpose of the message (to
offer advice based on the writer's experience). The writer is
also able to address specific teen concerns such as transportation for dates, fear of being at the beck and call of siblings,

and peer pressure. Again, the writer's voice, subject, and purpose become clear when the audience is clear.

Audience matters, then, because a clear sense of audience leads to better writing. It prevents us from writing generic papers that fill up pages without saying anything. It forces us to clarify the purpose of the paper and helps us to decide how much and what kind of information should be included. When we have identified an audience, we also know our relationship to that audience and therefore what tone of voice we should use in addressing those readers. In other words, audience is essential to good writing; and if we want our writing to matter to anyone, we have to take the needs of the reader into account and keep those needs in mind as we compose.

Chapter 2

Adjusting Style to Audience

Hi Susie!
Sue—
Dear Sue,
Dear Susan:

Dear Mrs. Gibbs:
Dear Sir or Madam:
Dear Subscriber:
Occupant:

In the course of a month's mail, it would not be unusual to find items addressed in all of the above ways arriving at the same house for the same person. Yet the style of address is completely different in each and depends on the relationship between the writer and the audience. The "Hi Susie!" writer probably knows Susie very well, and what follows will likely be a personal, friendly letter—an expressive piece of writing. The writer of "Occupant," on the other hand, obviously does not have the slightest idea who Susan Gibbs is. That greeting is probably leading to an informative letter about the neighborhood garbage pickup or a sale at a nearby store.

We make adjustments like these in our style every day. We do not speak to friends or family members in the same way that we address strangers or people in authority over us. We adjust our style to suit the needs and expectations of our audiences in the same way that we adjust our clothing for different occasions. (We do not wear a bathing suit to a formal dinner or a tuxedo to the beach.)

It is important to remember that we do this kind of adjusting naturally every day of our lives. The difficulty comes in transferring our speaking skills to our writing style. Many of us find this transfer difficult because the audience in writing is not standing in front of us providing immediate feedback to what we are saying. Instead, we have to imagine our readers and anticipate their responses. When the audience is a good friend, this task is easy; but when the audience is someone we do not know, this task demands skill and careful thought.

The Style Continuum

The adjustments we make for audience can be seen as moving along a continuum from a very personal to a more public, essay style depending on the relationship between writer and reader:

PERSONAL   PUBLIC

Self	Friends	Familiar	Composite
As	As	Audience	Audience
Audience	Audience		

Figure 2-1: The Style Continuum

As our relationship to the audience becomes more distant, we begin to change the tone of voice we use, the amount and kind of information we provide, and the mechanical features of style such as punctuation and spelling. We can see how audience affects style if we look at several stages of the continuum in more detail.

Self As Audience

Dear Diary,
  Sunday. Usual stuff. Dinner with THEM (!) again and I just felt as I always do. Must call J later.

The most personal kind of writing is that which we do for ourselves—notes that we make for our memories or for classes, the prewriting we do for a paper, the grocery and job lists we make to help us get our work done. These writings are seldom shared because of their private nature, although some diaries and personal journals have been published because of an interest in the writer or the historical events recorded by the writer. But for those of us who are not likely to become famous and who do not record historical events in our journals, the writing we do for ourselves either remains private or is revised into a more public form before it is shared.

The preceding example illustrates the characteristics of the personal style with self as audience:

Voice: The tone of voice we use in this kind of writing is personal, reflects our mood at that time, and does not adjust for anyone else; we do not try to curb our anger, for example, if we are mad at someone. This is the type of writing in which we can really be ourselves—warts and all.

Subject matter: This, too, is completely self-centered. We write about anything we like in any way we want. Often, as in the above example, there are vague references such as "Sunday," "stuff," and "THEM." Because we understand the subject completely, these references need no explanation.

Mechanics: Because we are the only readers for this prose, our grammar and punctuation may range from loose to idiosyncratic. We may suddenly abandon sentences in favor of lists. We may forget to signal the end of sentences or make single words stand alone with no context to help explain them, as "Sunday" does above. We may also use personal abbreviations for things and people ("J") that are meaningful only to us.

The informal nature of this writing, and the fact that it can be virtually indecipherable to anyone else, does not diminish its value for the writer. Journals are records of memories and experiences. Notebooks may contain information that will turn into a more public kind of writing later. Lists are handy reminders of the day's work. We should not underestimate the value of this style of writing just because of its private nature.

Friends As Audience

Dear Joy,

Long time no see. I guess neither of us is very good about writing. Sorry. I thought of you this week, though, because I'm applying for a job at your school. You know how we used to make fun of Mrs. Ryan, our Resident Director? Well, with any luck, kids'll be making fun of me next year. I want to be a Resident Director. Can you believe it?

Anyway, I'm applying for this job and wondered if you could share any information you might have about the dorm system or the school or even the person who's leaving if you know her. I have to write a letter of application so any info would be helpful.

You can send me stuff at the same old address or you can call me (collect even!). I hope you are well and hope you are having as much fun there as we did here. Talk to you soon.

Your old roomie,

Chris

Writing that we do to friends is also often quite personal and informal. But no matter how close we are to these readers, they still cannot read our minds, and so the writing takes on characteristics that are different from those found in writing for self.

The above letter illustrates the characteristics of the friendly style:

Voice: The voice for this writing is once again very personal. However, we usually assume some kind of role as we write that defines our relationship to our reader. We write using the voice of daughter, old friend, nephew, grandmother, loving husband. And how much of our self we reveal will depend on this role. In the letter above, Chris is speaking in the role of a former "roomie" who has lost touch with an old friend from whom she now needs a favor. Although the letter reflects some of her feelings, she has undoubtedly sorted through them and probably censored them somewhat. For example, she may not be sorry at all for losing contact with her friend but still recognizes that this is a polite thing to say if she wants her friend to help her. She may also feel very embarrassed about the long silence, but she does not dwell on it (as she might have in a diary entry she wrote while trying to make the decision to write the letter). In other words, for these readers, we often remove a few warts.

Subject matter: Topics covered in correspondence with friends usually focus on what we share. We write mostly to share news, and the bond of caring between the writer and the audience forms the basis for the discourse. In the above letter, Chris focuses on memories about school, making fun of Mrs. Ryan, and Joy's new school. Also, references are often made which would not be understood by a more distant audience ("same old address"), but these make sense to the friendly audience because of the reader's closeness to the writer.

Mechanics: Grammar and punctuation may still be somewhat nontraditional for this audience because of the conversational quality of the writing, but they will be conventional enough to make the passage clear to the reader. Thus, Chris's subjectless sentences ("Long time no see." and "Sorry.") are not inappropriate in this context, nor is her emphatic parenthetical remark (collect even!) or her slang (roomie). On the other hand, the shift toward more public writing can be seen in her use of paragraphs, transitions, and the letter format, none of which would be necessary in writing for self.

Although the style we use with a friend may be very informal and our mechanics may not follow strict rules of grammatical correctness, this letter is still a good piece of finished prose *for this audience.* Although it might be inappropriate for the kind of writing situations we will discuss later in this chapter, it is entirely appropriate in this one. To be too formal with friends, close family members, or peers would ruin a good piece of writing by making the writer sound phony and distant.

The Familiar Audience

Familiar audiences range from one-on-one correspondence, which is quite similar to writing for friends, to communication aimed at very large groups, which may be nearly as formal as that written for a composite audience (discussed in the next section). What these readers all have in common is that they can be identified by the writer. All the readers belong to a particular group, and so another way to describe this discourse is as "in-house" communiqués. The "house" may be quite small (as when I make comments on my students' papers) or quite large (as when a company sends out a memo to all of its employees). But in either case, the audience is limited and each of its members identified.

In addition, this style is different from that used with friends because our role as a writer is not personal but professional or social. We write as a member of the group. Thus, when I comment on students' papers, I write as a teacher, assuming a professional role, not as a personal friend. Similarly, when a company executive sends out a memo, the writer is speaking in that professional capacity as executive. A company executive who suddenly decided to send out memos about personal family matters, or personal opinions on political issues, would not be appreciated and probably not remain an executive for long.

Finally, this kind of writing is very time-bound. It usually refers to some event that is happening in the present and is usually quickly discarded after the communication is over. Some students may keep their writing folders and my comments when the class is over, but most will not; and the timely company memo will soon be found in the circular file.

Perhaps it would be helpful to look at an example of discourse in this style at both ends of the spectrum:

Sam—

This paper turned out very well. Your reason for wanting to become an environmental lawyer is very clear, and the ending about giving something back to the wilderness that has given you so much pleasure is really quite moving. Your personal introduction gets us involved in the essay right away. And the contrast between the general magazines you read as you grew up and the magazines you started to read as you became more involved in environmental issues serves as vivid support for your claim of involvement.

My only suggestion would be to explain more clearly what you mean by the job providing emotional, intellectual, and financial rewards. That is thrown in at the end and doesn't fit very well with the rest of the paper.

Good job overall. I'm very pleased with the way this paper developed through the drafts.

Jan

When I write comments on my students' papers, as in the above example, I am writing to a familiar audience. The reader is identified and known to me but is not a personal friend. My role is also clearly professional. I am writing as the teacher and focusing my comments on the writing. But the style is still conversational, as it might be with friends, and the mechanics are still somewhat loose, allowing for phrases such as "Good job overall" to stand alone.

When the familiar audience is larger, the style tends to become more formal and the information much more general:

TO: All Returning Students
FROM: Student Government Office
RE: Credit/No Credit System

When registration begins on March 3, you will find that a new option is available on your program card, called the credit/no credit system. Under this system, you can take courses without receiving a letter grade. The course is still recorded on your transcripts, but your course grade does not count toward your GPA.

However, you must *be careful* in exercising this option. You must earn at least a C in the course for the credit to count. You should also not sign up for credit/no credit if you are taking courses in your major or minor field. Credit/no credit courses will not count toward these requirements.

If you have any questions about this new option, please stop by the Student Government Office during the week of registration. We will be glad to help you decide what is best for you.

The last line of this communiqué clearly illustrates the difference the size of the group makes. As a teacher in a small class, I can give individual and certainly very specific instructions and examples to my students. The writer of this memo cannot because the audience is too large and the needs of the audience too diverse. Each student will need to come in for individual help. The writer can only outline the credit/ no credit option in the most general terms—just enough to inform people that the option exists and let them know how to get more help. Also, the mechanics have become standard, representing the public image of the university as an educational institution.

The above passages illustrate the characteristics of writing done for a familiar audience:

Voice: The voice in this kind of writing tends to be more "official," emphasizing a particular public role (student government staff, teacher, employer, club officer). How impersonal or official our voice is will depend on the size of the group, how well we know each member, and the status of the position we hold.

Subject matter: The subject matter for familiar audiences usually focuses on what the writer and reader share—registration, the student's writing, a change in company policy. Their common knowledge about the subject allows for many unexplained references similar to those found in writings for self and friends. The student government writer does not need to explain words such as "registration," "major," or "minor." In speaking to my student, I do not need to tell him what magazines he mentioned in his paper. Still, the subjects are not personal, but matters of professional or public concern.

Mechanics: Even though something is shared with a familiar audience, the relationship between the writer and reader is still more distant. Readers are much less likely to understand or tolerate idiosyncratic spelling or personal abbreviations. We must therefore observe enough of the standard rules for grammar and punctuation so the audience can follow what we are trying to say. In addition, we may need to be concerned about proper format for this audience—an office might want all of its in-house writing done in standard memo form, for example.

The Composite Audience

The composite audience is a group of general readers, all of whom cannot be identified in the way the employees of an organization or the students enrolled at a particular school

can. Usually the audience is so large and varied that only
profiles or composites of them can be formed, and we must
write to a group that essentially can only be imagined. Once
again this audience may range from a rather select, easily
imagined group, such as the readers of a local newspaper, to
a group that is huge and diverse, like the audience for *Reader's
Digest*.

There are many familiar kinds of writing done for composite
audiences: textbooks, newspapers, magazines, reference
books, and essays. It may seem that the audiences for these
writings could be defined as "any literate reader." But just
because all literate readers *could* read these pieces does not
make them the intended audience. Each of these has a more
specific target audience even though the discourse will probably reach many other people.

For example, the essays collected in "readers" for college
courses are meant to illustrate writing that is aimed at a
general reader. However, most of these essays were written
for much more specific audiences. First, these essays are
found in collections for college students; this means their
primary audience is the well-educated reader, not the general
public. Second, it is obvious in glancing through the table
of contents of one of these books that some of the essays will
be of great interest to some people and of little interest to
others. For example, an essay on sports will have a much
greater appeal to someone involved in competitive games
than to someone who finds them boring. Finally, most of
the essays come from magazines that have a very specific
readership; they were not written for the general reader, but
for the specific readers of *Ebony*, *Scientific American*, *Esquire*,
or *Seventeen*. In other words, just because most literate people
are *able* to read an essay does not mean that they have any
interest in doing so or that the authors would expect them
to. Similarly, textbooks, newspapers, and even encyclopedias
and dictionaries have target audiences for which they are
written.

The style of these writings can best be described as public—
that is, meant to be shared with a large group of readers who

are not known by the writer. This kind of writing has several characteristics:

Voice: The voice used is public, and generally reflects the conventions of the kind of writing we are doing. If we are writing a newspaper article or researched report, for example, the voice will be very objective.

Subject matter: The topics discussed are usually of general interest to the composite audience imagined by the writer. There are few references that would exclude readers or limit their understanding. The subject is explained and examined in a public way usually with the intention of providing information or personal insight.

Mechanics: Standard grammar, punctuation, spelling, and usage are usually the order of the day in this style. Progression through the writing is usually aided by logical keys to organization such as: first, second, finally; if/then; X therefore Y; not only/but also; or the who, what, when, where, why, how structure of a newspaper.

Illustrating the Continuum

Now we can look at how the style of a piece of writing would change as it moved along this continuum from personal to public. The writer, Don, is an avid racquetball player whose interest in the sport and experience managing a racquetball club have made him very concerned about safety. He wrote about this interest in a series of pieces he did for an advanced composition class. The following writings, then, all have the same subject (racquetball) and the same writer (Don). The audience, however, changes for each piece.

When Don first decided to write about racquetball, he began by listing ideas that could become part of his writing. This brainstorming was done only for himself.

Self As Audience: Brainstorming List

```
Events:  my accident
         Dan Woerner's accident--guilt
         people asking for my advice at the club--
            my responsibility
         AARA ruling on eyeguards
```

```
Opinions:  everyone should wear eyeguards
           AARA ruling should extend to all levels
           safety is not inconvenient or
                uncomfortable
           it is a dangerous sport without
                protection (stats on accidents)

Audience:  anyone who plays racquetball? (magazine)
           club owners? (newsletter)
           friends? (letter)
           newcomers? (on list of club rules)
```

Don made this list to try to recall all the information at his disposal. He has a considerable amount of personal experience to draw on, as well as professional experience as a club manager and a tournament player. Don also considers possible audiences and indicates that he understands that the paper would have to change for each one.

Notice the style of the writing. The voice is personal and reflects not only his own thoughts but his comments on those thoughts ("my responsibility" he notes about giving advice to club members). At this stage he is including everything he can think of even though all of these ideas could never be included in one piece of writing. He uses his own shorthand, his own emphasis, his own organization. This is personal and expressive writing for self, and yet the writer has produced a valuable checklist of ideas for later, more public writing.

Friends As Audience: Personal Letter

Shortly after Don learned to play racquetball from a friend, Mike, he had an accident on the court. Wearing eyeguards was one piece of advice his friend had not given him, and Don decided to share his hard-earned knowledge with his former teacher.

```
Dear Mike,

      Thanks for playing last week. I appreciate
the pointers. Racquetball has turned out to be a
lot of fun (now that I'm improving!).
```

I had a close call the other night. I was playing Tom, and he had some trouble returning one of my serves. I kept waiting for the return, but it never came. So, like a dummy, I turned around to see what happened. The next thing I knew, I was on the floor with blood all over my face. Tom thought he'd killed me, and I was ready to agree. The ball hit me right in the eye after Tom returned it. Thank goodness I was wearing my glasses. The frames shattered and cut me on the eyebrow, but I was lucky. I don't like to think about what would have happened if I had worn my contacts that night.

The thing was it happened so _fast_. There was nothing I could do. I felt helpless. But being a quick learner, I bought some eyeguards to use with my contacts. At least now I'm protected from the "freak accident."

Well, enough for now. After all those tips you gave me last week, I felt I owed you one. Pass this on to your next "student"--Don't take chances with your eyes! I think I was lucky to get a warning.

                              Your friend,
                              Don

Don has written a personal letter thanking his friend for the help, but also hinting that Mike could have told him more about the dangers of the sport during his lessons. Notice the voice in this letter. Don may be quite angry at Mike for not telling him to wear eyeguards, but has decided not to let that side of himself show. In other words, he has censored his feelings somewhat—he lets his friend know he was hurt, cautions him to warn others, but does not actually chastise the friend for the omission in his instructions.

The subject matter focuses on their shared interest in racquetball and their common interest in each other's safety. The good fellowship of the past week is used to establish a relationship that will allow the writer to give advice to his friend. References are made that would only be understood by them (the identity of Tom, for example, and the nature of Mike's tips), thus indicating that Mike is a close friend.

The mechanics are informal, as seen in the sentence structure ("Well, enough for now") and punctuation ("now that I'm improving!") as well as in the joking way in which he refers to himself as Mike's "student." This style is meant to renew the feelings of camaraderie that these two men shared so that Mike will take the letter seriously. If he can hear Don's familiar voice in the words of the letter, he may be more inclined to listen to his advice for both his own sake and that of his future "students." In other words, in dealing with a friendly audience, the personal, informal style can be an effective method of persuasion.

The Familiar Audience: Opinion Essay

Don's next writing about racquetball was done for his classmates. He decided to write an expressive piece about the Dan Woerner accident he had mentioned in his brainstorming list. The guilt he had mentioned after Dan's name comes through clearly in his writing.

> While racquetball is not a violent sport, it is not without its risks. The court is often crowded and the ball moves quickly--just the situation in which an eye injury can occur. While the American Amateur Racquetball Association has made eye protection mandatory for AARA-sanctioned tournaments, very little has been done to promote the use of eyeguards at the club level. Where the chance of injury exists and no standard is in effect to protect the public, the responsibility falls to those knowledgeable of the risks.

> My job at a local racquetball club puts me in just such a position of responsibility. Members at the club trust in my judgment and frequently seek my answers to their questions about the sport. Since I am also the current teaching pro, new members--especially beginners--often need my guidance.

These are responsibilities I take very seriously. Occasionally, however, I fail in making
beginners adequately aware of the importance of
eyeguards and the risks associated with the decision not to wear them. Usually a close call
prompts them to ask if "those things" are really
necessary. I always tell them, "Very much so--I
never set foot on the court without them!" Luck-
ily, no one was ever injured who hadn't been
warned.

Until Dan Woerner.

Dan was a new member--a beginner. I had only
spoken to him briefly a couple of times. Last
night Dan played for the fourth time. Ten minutes
into the match Dan was struck in the eye by a
racquetball . . . and he wasn't wearing any
eyeguards. There was some bleeding in the white
of his eye, and there was bruising on his cheek,
nose, and eyebrow. The vision in the eye was
blurred and erratic, but we haven't yet learned
the extent of his injury.

I tell myself that people are often suspi-
cious when someone they don't know tells them,
"You need this." It could be hype or aggressive
salesmanship. I like to give people time to get
to know me, so they realize that I am motivated
by their personal welfare, not just the urge to
move inventory.

Dan Woerner didn't have that time. He didn't
have the chance to refuse to wear eyeguards, because I didn't make the effort to sell them. What
is worse, I didn't even warn him about the risk
of not wearing eyeguards when playing racquetball
--something that I personally would never do.

In this, I failed Dan Woerner. I only hope
he can see his way clear to forgive me.

This time, Don has written a more public and fuller expression of his feelings about eye accidents. It was one thing to
have a close call himself and quite another to feel responsible
for someone else's close call. As Mike had failed to warn

him, he had failed to warn someone else, and this essay is
a powerful expression of the guilt he feels.

Don knew everyone in the class so we were a familiar
audience to him, but we were not personal friends. Don had
to take our needs into account. He had to consider that some
of us had never played racquetball, were not aware of the
risks, and would not understand why he would feel responsible
for someone else's safety. He therefore takes the time in
the first part of the paper to explain why the responsibility
for warning players rests on him and to set up the story of
Dan Woerner.

In terms of style, then, Don's voice is conversational, but
it is also professional, since he is speaking as an authority of
racquetball and as an employee of a racquetball club. He
uses personal pronouns, but the "I" signifies the selection of
his professional role.

In terms of subject matter, Don is careful to fill in the
details of the situation for his audience so we understand the
significance of this experience for him. We are filled in on
the idea that the sport can cause injury, that there are no
set rules to follow about eyeguards, that Don usually takes
his responsibility to advise players about the dangers seriously,
and that he feels he played a clear role in Dan's accident.

In terms of mechanics, Don's style has become slightly
more formal in that he is now writing an essay. Because of
the more public nature of the audience, Don follows most
rules of standard grammar and usage. But the familiarity of
the audience still allows for him to use a single phrase as a
paragraph for dramatic effect.

The Composite Audience: Magazine Article

Don's last writing about this topic was a persuasive essay
aimed at a composite audience of racquetball club owners,
employees, and members. He imagined the essay appearing
in a national racquetball magazine where it might also reach
a wider audience of players who were not club members. He

based his composite on his own boss, himself, his co-workers, and the members and players he knew.

Mandatory eyeguards for racquet sports is an issue whose time has come. Given the number of injuries occurring yearly and the ease with which most of them can be prevented, now is the time to take a stand and require eye protection across the board at the professional, tournament, and club level.

In the past, eye protection was the responsibility of the individual. When people had an option, they often chose not to wear eyeguards for a variety of reasons. Eyeguards were bulky, unattractive, and in some cases ineffective. These problems have, for the most part, been eliminated. Eyeguards today offer excellent protection, are comfortable to wear, and come in a variety of styles and colors to suit personal tastes. The only reason why most players today will not wear eyeguards is the fact that they are not required. It is this "personal choice" philosophy which leads to the 70,000 eye injuries in racquet sports each year.

Dramatic changes in the games during the last ten years have made this philosophy dangerous. The ball composition has changed from "dead" to "lively." Racquet construction bears only a slight resemblance to the wooden or fiberglass racquets of yesterday. Today's racquets come in midsize and oversize versions crafted of high-tech materials such as graphite, boron, kevlar, and ceramic. They are capable of generating power in the hands of an amateur today that yesterday's professionals could only dream about. As a result, the game has changed from one of slow, patient rallies emphasizing control, to one of drives and "kills" emphasizing power. It is unrealistic to expect any but the most gifted of athletes to have reactions capable of avoiding injury.

All of these factors add up to one inescapable fact. Attitudes about eyeguards have not

kept pace with the risks involved in playing
court sports. Modern technology has led to in-
creased risks, while attitudes and information
have lagged behind. However, this is a trend
which can easily be reversed. Where technology
has created a problem, it has now created a solution. Current research shows that the greatest
amount of protection is available in the form of
eyeglass-type frames fitted with polycarbonate
lenses. They are light, comfortable, and inexpen-
sive. And racquet sports' sanctioning bodies have
endorsed the push for safety by making eye protection mandatory for sanctioned tournament play.

The greatest limitation of these endorse-
ments is the "sanctioned tournament play" clause.
These regulatory bodies only have the authority
to influence their own tournament players, a
minority in the larger body of recreational
players. To be effective, eye protection must be
mandatory at the club level.

Racquet sports have much to gain from this
ruling. Foremost would be the prevention of many
--if not most--of the 70,000 eye injuries per
year suffered by racquet sports participants.
Public perception of court sports would be im-
proved as the number of eye injuries declined,
perhaps increasing play as a result. True, there
will be some loss of players who simply will not
play if required to wear eyeguards. But, as Chuck
Leve points out in National Racquetball, February
1986, "the truth is that racquetball is damaged
a great deal more by eye injuries than by those
few . . . who would bypass [play] because eyeguards were mandatory" (p. 2).

It is clear that there is widespread support
within the industry, the medical field, and the
sport itself for a mandatory eyeguard ruling at
all levels of play. It's time the local club owners join in to support an idea whose time has come.

Notice how Don has returned to his original brainstorming
list of events and opinions to construct this essay and to find

his audience. He has now written a very public piece, to be read nationwide, and to call people to action on this issue.

The voice here is quite public. Although Don has personal experience to draw on, his particular accident now becomes part of a statistic of 70,000 accidents. Although he personally feels responsible for helping people make a wise decision about eye safety, he speaks of this in terms of a "personal choice philosophy." Rather than relying on his own opinions for authority, he uses his knowledge of equipment, the history of the sport, and the current trends in the sport to support his assertions. His voice is persuasive, but he tries to make the opinion universal rather than personal.

The subject matter is interesting to the composite audience. He tries to provide them with information on the subject of safety and insight into the solution to the problem of eye injuries. Again, he uses solid information to back up his claims.

In terms of mechanics, Don is following standard grammar and usuage guidelines. His paragraphs are also fully developed, and his arrangement is logical with clear transitions leading from one point to the next.

The Continuum Revisited

Just as the three purposes of writing (expressive, persuasive, and informative) are not separate, but overlap and often appear in the same piece of writing, so the four styles we have discussed describe tendencies, not absolute characteristics.

For example, notes that high school students pass to each other in the halls are written in a style that is very much like a diary (that is, written for self), but one that a close friend is invited to share. Similarly, notes taken for a class, although written only for us, are probably still meaningful for other people taking the same class (although they may need some help with our shorthand and abbreviation systems).

Friendly audiences often blend with familiar readers when we write a discourse such as interdepartmental memos. We may be friends with everyone in the department and share a common bond and interest that characterizes writing for friendly readers, but the subject would be strictly professional. Reports meant only for a limited group of colleagues or peers would also fall into this category.

The composite audience may also be a mixture of familiar and unknown readers. When the head of a regional or national organization writes a newsletter to all members, the writer undoubtedly knows a good number of the members personally, but certainly not all of them, and the ranks might change too quickly to have a complete list of all members.

Remember that these styles describe a continuum, not a series of steps. Each audience is different and demands that the writer select the appropriate voice, subject matter, and style to suit the readers' needs. Each occasion for writing demands that the writer make wise choices. These descriptions are meant to serve only as a guide, not as a rule book.

Also, this continuum is not meant to be progressive in terms of the value or quality of the writing. Each writing style is equally effective if used in appropriate situations. There is nothing inherently "better" about public prose. In fact, it would be valueless and perhaps even harmful if used in the wrong situation.

Finally, let me emphasize that the style a writer selects for a particular audience must be sustained throughout the piece. It is not enough simply to signal the intended audience and the level of formality in the opening paragraph. The tone set in the beginning of the paper must be consistent throughout. When this rule is not followed, the result is nonsense, as the following computer letter illustrates:

Dear Jan Youga,

Here's a great money-saving and BONUS GIFT offer for you, if you act quickly! Now you can receive either Bonified Quartz watch you see illustrated above when you subscribe to THE MAGAZINE at incredible savings!

This splendidly designed timepiece, with its genuine leather band, has been created expressly for THE MAGAZINE. Its slim styling and elegant face make this watch a perfect complement to your own fine wardrobe, Jan Youga. It is a watch you can wear every day, but you will be especially pleased to display it at important business and social events.

If you appreciate style, taste, and elegance, you will want to own this Bonified Quartz timepiece. It cannot be bought at any Bloomington jeweler for any price. But you can receive one as our SPECIAL GIFT to you, Jan Youga, when you subscribe to THE MAGAZINE.

The authors here are attempting to make this letter personal by inserting my name and specific personal information such as the town in which I live. These attempts fail miserably because the rest of the letter is so obviously intended for thousands of other readers. For example, if the watch is supposed to complement my fine wardrobe, I am not likely to select the man's watch that is "illustrated above." This combination of formal and informal styles makes the letter sound ridiculous. And the occasional insertion of my name is not enough to make the letter audience-specific. A student paper, such as that found in Chapter 1, which pretends to address "people today" in the first paragraph but goes on to talk about parents buying cars for teenagers, will be equally ineffective.

PART TWO

Audience Attitudes

Dialogue overheard between two 10-year-old boys:

Boy 1: Can you stay over at my house Tuesday?
Boy 2: I don't know. I'll have to ask.
Boy 1: Well, go ahead.
Boy 2: Not now, stupid. Mom just got home from work. She'll
for sure say no now. And besides, I'll ask Dad first. He
says yes to everything.

Boy 2 is demonstrating the very sophisticated skill of audience
analysis: he knows when his audience is most likely to be
receptive and which of his two audiences is the easier mark.
The boy knows that for questions like "staying over," it is
better to ask Dad first and let him talk to Mom, and that
when he needs to ask Mom for something himself, it is not
wise to bother her when she first gets home from work.

As writers, we need to use this same skill ourselves—we
need to consider what will make our audience receptive to
our message and how different audiences will receive the
same message in different ways. In other words, in addition
to determining our purpose and the right style for a particular
audience, we also need to anticipate the attitude these readers
will have toward what we are saying. Will they be receptive
to our message, or are we telling them things they would
rather not hear? Will their attitude toward us be friendly, or

will they be looking at us as the enemy? The stance we think our audience will take will help us to shape what we say and how we say it. If our audience is antagonistic, for example, we would only make matters worse by starting out with inflammatory remarks about how stupid people are who disagree with us.

In the next four chapters, we will examine a number of possible attitudes that audiences might have as they approach a piece of writing and how those attitudes influence what the writers say.

Chapter 3

Sharing Ourselves with the Willing Listener

Conversation at a high school class reunion:

> Woman 1: Karen?
>
> Woman 2: Marsha! How are you? You haven't changed . . .
>
> Woman 1: . . . a bit. Yes, I know. I think I've heard that fifty times tonight. I'm not so sure I like the idea of still looking 17, especially when I see those old prom pictures. So what are you doing now?
>
> Woman 2: I'm going to school again.
>
> Woman 1: School! You always hated school.
>
> Woman 2: I know, but after 10 years as a bank teller, I decided I knew enough to *run* the bank. So, I'm in college now, getting a degree in finance. How about you?

These two women are good examples of *willing listeners*. They have something in common—high school—and can use this as a basis for their conversation. Their talk that evening will probably be filled with stories about themselves, their families, and their jobs. If the conversation is long enough, they may start to reminisce and swap stories about the good old days. They will also very likely exchange more opinions—about the importance of a satisfying job, about the need for education, about how their high school friends have turned out, about the reunion idea itself. They could well go on for hours!

However, they will probably be somewhat careful about the topics they discuss. They will not want to bring up subjects about which they might seriously disagree because that might ruin the evening. They will also probably not swap tall tales. They might exaggerate a little about their careers or the angelic qualities of their children, but their talk will concentrate on true-life experiences and genuine feelings and opinions.

The willing listener, then, is friendly, sometimes a new acquaintance who is trying to get to know us and other times an old friend who is just keeping up with the news of our lives. And the stance of the willing listener is one of acceptance: we are not being judged so much as we are being discovered — or rediscovered.

Writing done for such an audience will be read almost eagerly, as the reader is anxious to know something about us, our lives, or our opinions. The writer's job is to share something honestly with these readers, for they will assume that we are sincere and are willingly participating in this communication.

The two most common kinds of writing that we do for willing listeners can be seen in the above dialogue. These two women are swapping stories and sharing personal opinions.

Swapping Stories

Narratives are simply stories about experiences we have had that we think will interest others. We are also trying to make some point in the story—we learned something by the experience or were somehow changed by it. People read these tales because they are interested in us or are entertained by the story itself. We do not expect our readers to judge us, to say that what we did was right or wrong, but simply to listen and learn something about who we are, where we came from, and why this experience was significant enough to be preserved in our memories. We also probably hope that they can relate to the experience in some way and recall something similar in their own lives.

Narratives are often one of the first assignments in composition classes, and they serve a similar purpose to the stories shared by the women at the reunion — they help students get to know something about each other. But in the process of reading narratives, we find out not only about specific people, but about different life-styles, different parts of the world, and different ways in which people have responded to various situations. Narratives can therefore be a learning, as well as an entertaining, experience.

The following student paper is an example of a narrative that was written for a college composition class. The purpose of the assignment was to help students get acquainted by sharing something about their backgrounds.

Sample Narrative

> We had company every Sunday when I was a kid. My mom had five sisters, and it seemed like one if not all of them spent Sundays at our house. It was a big family deal--all the women around the stove in the kitchen, all the men around the TV in the family room, and all the kids around the toys in the basement.
>
> Of all the roles I've had to play in my life, being a kid was one of my biggest failures. It didn't take long for me to get tired of the toys and my idiot cousins, and I'd soon sneak back upstairs and sit on the landing so I could hear the women talk. I didn't understand most of their conversations; they always talked about things like pregnancies, hysterectomies, and mastectomies--and always in whispers.
>
> One Sunday when all five aunts were visiting and I was in my usual perch at the top of the stairs, my mother began to talk about a young neighbor girl who was "in trouble," and suddenly she paused, and then sounds, like words, began to come out of her mouth which I couldn't understand at all. I had a school teacher at that time who could do the same thing, and I knew my mother was speaking another language. I was sure my

school teacher was a saint who had a special gift
from God, and I was thrilled that my mother had
the same sacred privilege.

That night when all the aunts had gone home,
I told my mom about my great discovery. I was so
excited the words just poured out of me:

"I heard you talking, Mom. You have a gift
just like my teacher. What language is it, Mom?
How did you learn it? Can I learn it, too? Can I
have this gift?"

Her slap stung my cheek. I'd been eavesdrop-
ping. I knew that was wrong and stood waiting
for more just punishment. But instead she said,
"Gift! Gift! You stupid girl. You think it's a
gift? It's a curse, I tell you! Do you know what
it's like to talk like this, to be a backward
foreigner, have people laugh at you all the
time?"

She took me by the shoulders and brought
her face down to just a few inches from mine.
"You're an American. A city girl and an American.
Do you understand?"

I didn't until much later, but I never mentioned my mother's gift again.

This simple story was the writer's attempt to share with
her classmates why she felt separated from her own ethnic
background and what she saw as part of her own identity.
But there is no preaching here; she does not end by chastising
parents who do not share their "gifts" with their children.
She also does not ask for sympathy (although we may feel
some) by bemoaning her monolingual state. Her point is not
to preach or to cast blame, but simply to share an interesting
and important experience with her new classmates, one that
may cause both children and parents to reflect on how people
develop a sense of identity.

Her classmates listened willingly because they wanted to
hear some information about her. They did not respond by
taking sides, either agreeing or disagreeing with the mother's

position. Instead, in a discussion that followed the reading of this paper, several students told of similar incidents or told how ethnic heritage was celebrated in their families. In other words, their willingness to listen went beyond just wanting to know the author; they wanted to relate the incident to their own lives.

Voicing Opinions

The women at the reunion not only swapped stories, but also shared personal opinions. *Personal opinion essays* are ways for the writer to share a point of view about a particular aspect of life with people who care about what the writer thinks. Topics vary as much as people's opinions do and may be something as simple as a favorite color or as profound as the existence of God.

In order to understand this form of writing, we perhaps first need to say what it is not; that is, it is *not persuasive*. We are not trying to convince someone that red is the only beautiful color in the world or that God exists. In this situation, we are letting someone know how we feel about something in the same way that we would tell a new friend that we like Humphrey Bogart movies or chocolate chip cookies. We are stating a preference, a belief that is a part of who we are or that helps to explain why we think or act in a particular way. Again, the point of this discourse is to share personal information in the hope that it will help people understand or relate to us (or to people like us) better.

As in the narrative, the audience for this essay agrees to listen willingly because of an interest in us or in our topic. But if we lose sight of the fact that this is just an exchange of personal information and we begin trying to impose our opinions on our readers, the trust set up between the writer and the audience is broken. Readers who came to the paper willing to listen will quickly become critical or even antagonistic if they feel we are trying to force them to share our opinions.

To get a sense of the difference between expressing an opinion to willing listeners and forcing an opinion on them, we can look at the following two statements:

1. I would never give candy to my children. It is bad for their health. Any parent who would fill an Easter basket with chocolate bunnies and marshmallow eggs is unfit to raise a child.

2. I've found that a lot of sugar makes Jimmy hyperactive, so I try not to let him have too much. I know it's hard on him, though, especially at holidays when other children have so much.

Even a parent who does not fill the Easter basket with bunnies would find it difficult to respond positively to statement 1 because of the tone of the writer. For that writer there is only one right way of doing things and everyone who does not agree is wrong. Surely there is more to judging the fitness of a parent than whether candy is part of the child's diet. The only way to answer such a statement is to agree just to keep the peace or to fight back. The statement automatically puts the audience on the defensive.

In statement 2, however, the audience is not expected to agree, and no judgments are made about people who might disagree. The parent is simply sharing an opinion that it is better for this child, Jimmy, not to have too much sugar. The statement is also not extreme, and so there is nothing to trigger a hostile reaction from the audience. Not all sugar is bad, just too much of it; not all children should give it up, but just this one. The second speaker, then, respects the stance of the willing listener and does not overstep the bounds by being pushy. In other words, willing listeners trust that we simply want to say something about who we are and what we think. If that trust is broken by our attempts to tell them who *they* ought to be or what *they* ought to think, they no longer have any obligation to listen to us willingly.

Now, let us look at the opening paragraphs of two student papers that are addressed to willing listeners.

Example 1

I often feel frustrated when trying to articulate something of my Christian belief. Either I end up claiming that my belief in God goes against all my reason, but that I somehow still believe; or I turn all scripture into one fantastic metaphor, guiding me toward some unattainable goal symbolized by "heaven" or "the Kingdom of God." On the one hand, I think I'm on the verge of becoming a fanatic, and on the other, I'm convinced I'm a true atheist. Yet neither of these explanations of my faith satisfies me. Instead they keep me defining and redefining my Christianity, in hopes that someday my faith will not only guide me toward some more purposeful life, but also help me articulate the "greater than thou" experience I have with God.

Example 2

Why do I run? People ask me that question all the time, and I'm never certain what to say. To clear the table first, I believe we can skip the obvious reasons: physical fitness, losing weight, longer life, and guiltless eating. We can also skip the idea that it's a fad; you know the type: "Oh, my gosh, Bessie! The Joneses are jogging. Pitch the rackets and get me some Nikes." These reasons may account for most of the people we see pounding the pavement every day. But the truly insane, addicted runners like me have another reason—something called a "runner's high." Let's face it—running is a drug.

Both of these writers are dealing with controversial topics that many people have strong feelings about. They are also trying to share their opinion about these topics, but to do it in such a way that the ideas are expressions of personal experience and belief, not mandates for proper behavior in others or demands for agreement. The listener's own opinions are respected, not threatened.

The authors accomplish this feat through different techniques. The first writer's stance is unthreatening because of her own frustration in trying to articulate her belief. She is still struggling and is, therefore, in no position to try to push her beliefs off on anyone else. This admitted weakness makes her ideas essentially harmless to believers and nonbelievers alike, although both sides may wish to rush in to "save her."

She may be ripe for persuasion herself, but she is not in a position to try to persuade anyone else yet. We can, therefore, listen willingly without feeling that she is attempting to do more than talk to us about this struggle.

The second author disarms us in a different way—through humor. Although he may be addicted to running, he is able to laugh at himself and his subject so that we immediately know he will not try to convince us that running is essential for our health and well being. If this were the case, he would certainly not end with the idea that running is a drug. His humor makes it clear that he is only sharing his personal opinion about how this sport has become a necessary part of his own life.

Sharing with a willing listener can be a very challenging position to maintain. When we are expressing opinions, we like to have people confirm our beliefs and reassure us that our opinions are valid. So we may easily lapse into trying to justify rather than explain, trying to persuade rather than inform.

One trick to avoiding this is to remember the situation of the women at the reunion. We can imagine that we are on a trip and that we have just met someone and will be spending several hours with this person. We want to pass the time pleasantly because the person seems nice and it will make the trip go faster. During the conversation, an issue comes up. We want to talk about it, and our fellow traveler, a willing listener, wants to hear what we have to say. But we do not know if this person shares our opinion, and we do not want to make the trip unpleasant by alienating this person or by starting an argument. We simple want to address the issue honestly, explain our view strictly as a matter of personal opinion, and make it clear that this person is free to agree or disagree. If we can imagine a situation such as this and keep a picture of this audience in our minds, we can usually explain our opinion without becoming persuasive and violating the expectations of the willing listener.

Writing meant for willing listeners, as I said earlier, is often used at the beginning of composition classes to give students a chance to get to know each other and to write from personal experience. It is also found in booklets made for class reunions in which each person provides an update on "life since graduation," or in letters that we send at holiday times to share the news of the year.

In a more formal form it is found in memoirs and autobiographies in which people tell the stories of their lives. In books such as these, the authors often express opinions about what happened to them, but since the experiences are unique and personal, seldom is their motivation to change the opinion of their readers. Similarly, just as a family member would follow the events of our lives with interest, it is also common for certain professional writers to develop a following of willing listeners who will read whatever these authors write. The readers become interested in the authors as people and want to keep track of the writers' experiences and feelings. E. B. White's essays and Madeleine L'Engle's journals are good examples, as well as the currently popular books of Bill Cosby.

Chapter 4

Persuading Others

Sometimes our aim is not just to share our opinions but to persuade others to agree with us. When our purpose is to persuade, we can generally anticipate three audience stances: the nodder, or person we are sure will agree with our position; the fence sitter, or person who has not decided on the issue yet and perhaps does not really care about it; and the antagonist, or person who we know opposes our position. Each of these audience stances demands a different approach from the writer.

The Nodder

Nodders are already on our side. We do not need to convince them that our issue is important or tell them what stand they should take. The question then is, if these readers already care about our topic and completely agree with our opinion, why would we want to write to them?

One reason is that we may want something more from them than just assent. Perhaps we need for them to act on their beliefs and to support the cause in some specific way. Another reason is that these people may need a little pep talk to assure them that we are all still "in this together."

Whatever our specific motivation for reaffirming our shared belief with these readers, we can assume that they will be receptive, and this makes our job a little easier. We can approach these readers confident that they share our concern and will probably be willing to help us if they can.

Still, our approach to persuading the nodder must be adjusted to suit our specific purpose. If our goal is to gain more support for the cause, probably a friendly nudge in the right direction will do, as when a friend calls to remind us that we promised we would help with a party and asks if we would mind being in charge of the decorations. The persuasion here can be gentle since the speaker already has the tacit agreement of the audience to help in some way.

On the other hand, if our goal is to give our readers a pep talk, the persuasive devices may not be gentle at all. A nodding audience is a perfect opportunity to state our position in the strongest terms possible and to get our readers fired up about the issue. The writer does not need to hold back, because the audience will agree with even the most extreme statements. An environmental lawyer speaking to a group of wildlife preservationists does not need to be subtle.

For example, the following two pieces of writing concerned a month-long study of Russia conducted by a church for its members. One involves simply reminding certain members of an obligation, while the other tries to get the congregation fired up about upcoming events.

The Gentle Nudge

Dear Bob,

You are probably aware that for the last twelve years, the Social Ministry Committee of our church has sponsored an annual mission study. This year's study will focus on Russia and will include four special church services, four special adult education classes, and a Russian dinner the last Sunday of the month.

As a new member of this committee, you will have a special role to play in planning and organizing the study. There are several projects we need someone to take charge of, and we want to give you a choice as to which one you want to tackle.

As an active member of this church, you realize how important it is for us to share responsibility and the work load for a project like this. We hope you also remember how rewarding last year's study was and will want to make this one equally successful.

One of the project coordinators will be contacting you soon to find out what you would like to do to help with this important church event. If you need more information to help you decide, please call me. I have lots of suggestions.

Sincerely,

Dave Sawyer

Both men have a commitment to their church's activities which include organizing this annual event. There is an acknowledged mutual dependence here; they need each other and are likely to get help from each other because of that need. Still, that help cannot be taken for granted; the audience must be reminded of this mutual obligation. Thus, Dave mentions that this is an annual event which the reader has participated in and enjoyed before, and that it is always the responsibility of committee members to help. However, he does offer Bob a choice about which activity he wants to take charge of. The writer is not anticipating a negative response to this request; he is simply reminding the reader of a tacit agreement they have to help the church when it is in need.

The Pep Rally Approach

Notice published in the church bulletin after the Russian study has ended:

USSR MISSION STUDY

The January Mission Study was eventful and inspirational. Attendance at adult nurture classes and at the mission dinner were the largest ever. We all had a great time and learned a good deal about Russia in the process.

But even though the study has ended, our opportunities have not. Plans are being made for a trip to a Russian Orthodox service in Chicago for their Easter service which is the week *after* ours. The trip will include

—a tour of the Russian Orthodox Church

    —a meeting with Father Blake who spoke at the dinner
    —a night at the homes of church families
    —Easter Eve and Day services
    —more samplings of Russian food and culture!

Contact the church office for more information or to make reservations. Don't let your commitment to this study end with the month. Call today!

This writing goes beyond the goal of just reminding someone about an obligation. The writer is trying to rekindle the enthusiasm that was undoubtedly present at the weekly studies and the dinner. Rather than just telling readers about the trip, the writer reminds the readers of the enthusiastic support the study received and lists all the benefits of taking the trip. The description is not complete, however. It is meant to pique interest and to get people to call the church office for more information.

From these two examples, we can see the wide range of approaches that might be successful with the nodder. Whatever strategy we use, however subtle or blatant we might be, we can count on assent. And if we choose the right approach, we can get the specific kind of support we want.

The Fence Sitter

If the audience agrees with our stand, we can be very firm in our opinion and build on what we know are commonly held values. But if the readers have not made up their minds yet, the persuasive task is more challenging. The writer needs to capture the readers' interest in the issue first and then convince them to see the issue in a particular way.

In general, interest is generated by involvement. We are drawn to things because we can relate to them in some way. A good persuasive device, then, is to make the readers feel that this issue relates to their lives, that it is important to them. Once we have captured their interest, we can then go on to try to make them agree with us through emotional or logical appeals.

One way to capture the audience's interest is to paint a

vivid picture of the issue. In the following paper, notice how the student begins with a vivid description of a dying animal, an image that cannot help but inspire compassion and arouse interest, before she goes on to explain what the issue is.

Sample Persuasive Essay

When I was 14 years old, my dog Angel was caught in a steel-jaw leghold trap. The sharp teeth of the trap ripped her tender flesh and shattered the bones of her small leg. When I found her, she was covered with drying blood; her teeth were broken from gnawing on the trap, and a sharp bone protruded through her matted fur. After she had endured this needless pain and confusion for more than 12 hours, death finally released Angel from her torment.

The saddest part of this story is that Angel is not alone in her fate. Twenty-five million animals are captured every year--13 million in the United States and Canada alone. The trapped animals suffer unimaginable anguish, thirst, hunger, freezing cold, and exhaustion. They often tear their flesh, break their teeth, or fracture their bones in an effort to escape. Many chew off their own limbs to get away.

The intended victims of the traps are "fur-bearing" animals like beavers, lynx, squirrels, wolves, arctic foxes, red foxes, muskrats, and raccoons, whose pelts are used for coats. Unfortunately, other less desirable animals also fall prey to the cruel jaws. It is estimated that two of these so-called "trash" animals are killed for each furbearing one. Geese, ducks, songbirds, eagles, owls, porcupines, and family pets are considered "trash," as are many endangered species like spotted cats and giant otters.

Proponents of the traps disregard the need-less suffering of the innocent animals. As a representative of the American Fur Resources Institute once said, "Until the animal can talk to me in our language, I don't believe we can

say he feels pain." However, many people's con-
sciences cause them to look beyond the language
barrier and recognize the wide terrified eyes,
broken bodies, and shrill whimpers as definite
signs of pain.

Leghold traps were once used to catch
poachers and escaped slaves. But long ago, people
realized how cruel the traps were and so pro-
hibited their use against humans. Fifty-nine
nations--including Austria, Chile, Denmark,
Norway, Switzerland, and West Germany--have completely outlawed the use of leghold traps. But
the United States, a country that prides itself
on being fair and just, still allows their use,
even though 78 percent of the American people
oppose them.

American fur traders claim banning leghold
traps would harm the fur industry. But other
countries have turned to soft-catch, box, and
instant-kill traps without lowering their fur
supplies. Another complaint of the trappers in
the United States is that these alternative traps
are more expensive. They would rather save money
than keep innocent animals from suffering unbear-
able torment.

Finally, at long last, people are starting
to realize how much animals have suffered at the
hands of trappers. House Bill 1797, which would
bar the use of these traps, was introduced into
the United States Congress on August 3. If enough
people show support for the bill, perhaps the
reign of the steel-jaw leghold traps will come
to an end.

Please act now by sending the enclosed postcard to your representative today!

Analysis of Persuasive Techniques

This writer uses several kinds of persuasion to get her audience off the fence. First, as I said, she *paints a vivid picture*
of the dying animal to arouse the interest of her readers.

Second, she establishes her own *credibility* through her firsthand experience with these traps. She describes her memories vividly so the audience will see the pain not only of the animal but of a 14-year-old girl losing a beloved pet. Even people who do not own pets or who are not animal lovers do not wish to see animals suffer and can sympathize with the young girl. In addition, she shows that she has been concerned about this issue for a long time. She became aware of the problem as a child, and now as an adult she is informed on the issue and knows the proper way (the House bill) to act on her convictions.

The writer is also using various kinds of *emotional appeals*. Paragraphs 1 and 2 focus on pity, but she wants more than that response from her readers. By paragraph 4, she is trying to make the audience feel angry and indignant enough to act. In paragraph 5 she appeals to pride, and in 6 she makes it clear that there are alternatives to the deadly device. After arousing all of these feelings, she gives a clear indication of how she wants this energy channeled—send in that postcard.

Finally, the writer is using *logical appeals*. She includes statistics on the number of animals killed and the number of Americans who already support abolishing the traps. She includes lists of "trash" animals and countries which prohibit the use of the devices. She is well informed in addition to being emotionally involved.

All of these devices are aimed at persuading the audience to make a commitment and to act. She uses a variety of appeals so that she can reach more people, since some will be convinced by logic while others will never need to read beyond the first emotional paragraph. That opening paragraph, though, is her way of getting all of her readers involved, of catching their attention. The other devices, then, help to sustain that interest and to appeal to specific kinds of readers.

The Antagonist

Finally, if the audience disagrees with us and we actually take up the challenge to try to make people see the other side, the job is formidable, to say the least. In general, people adamantly opposed to something will not change their minds after reading just one piece of writing, and it is rather naive to think that they will. Often, advice about writing persuasive essays seems to assume that if we just have a strong argument, anticipate the objections of our opponent, and present our opinion in a logical, organized fashion, the reader will have no choice but to change sides.

This idea is, of course, ridiculous because it denies the complexity of the human mind and human emotions. We all recognize that some of the beliefs we hold are irrational or sentimental or illogical, but that does not stop us from hanging on tenaciously to every one of them. We are often especially attached to long-standing beliefs that we associate with our identity or our self-image.

Still, a piece of writing aimed at an antagonistic audience may be one in a series of writings the reader has seen lately, all of which may be working to make the reader reconsider the issue. These readings combined with some experiences or conversations with friends who also disagree with the reader on this issue may begin to work to change our antagonist's mind. In this case, there may be some hope that our side will get a fair hearing.

Additional Persuasive Techniques

Assuming then that we are willing to take on this task, we can employ several important strategies to help make the antagonistic reader listen to what we have to say, even if our paper alone will not decide the issue in our favor.

The most important of these strategies is to "walk a mile" in the reader's shoes. We must be able to *look at the issue from the opponent's point of view*. This perspective will help us anticipate what kinds of appeals will work best and what objections the reader will have to what we say. One of the best prewriting exercises we can do to prepare for this kind of a paper is to try to explain to ourselves what the opposition's position is by listing all the points our adversaries would make if they were arguing this issue from their side. When we have outlined their position, we can begin to analyze what the underlying values and assumptions of this position are. These then become a basis for our appeal.

Second, we must *try to establish some common ground,* something that we share with the opposition. It may seem that two opposing sides could not possibly have anything in common. But we should never forget that, if nothing else, we can always be sure that opponents share a concern for the issue itself. Even anti- and pro-abortion groups share a common concern for the life of the fetus. Anti-abortion groups may argue for the value of life per se, while the pro-abortion groups may argue that the value of the life must be connected to the child's being wanted and properly loved and cared for once that child is born, but both groups value life. Similarly, both pro- and anti-capital punishment groups share a concern for justice and the quality of our legal system.

Third, we need to consider how to *disarm the reader.* If the reader approaches the text as an opponent, ready to fight, we have little hope of getting our message across. We need to find an approach that will set the reader at ease and put the audience in a listening frame of mind. This is very difficult to do, but we have already seen some examples of how to approach this task in the opinion essays. The writers of these essays disarmed the readers by *using humor* and by *approaching the subject uncertainly,* as if the writer were still exploring the issue. In the traps essay above, the writer used a strong *emotional appeal* to get the readers involved before they even knew what the issue was.

All these writers were also illustrating another technique for disarming the reader—*personalizing the issue.* If we can convince the reader that, at least *in some cases,* we may be right, that takes the issue out of the area of black and white and begins to move the reader toward a more qualified statement of belief that at least partially accounts for our side. In one piece of writing and working with an adamant opponent, that would be quite an accomplishment.

Sample Persuasive Essay

The example we will examine is on a favorite student topic—Greek life. The student knows that most of her readers have strong negative feelings about sororities and are not likely to listen with open minds to her defense of the Greek system. Notice how she works to include the opposition's point of view, to establish common ground, and to disarm the reader through a personal and emotional approach.

    Independent. That's how I felt when I first
came to college. I had not been unhappy at home,
but I had been looking forward to the freedom of
being on my own ever since I could remember. I
was delighted to find that my roommate in the
dorm had a boyfriend with an apartment and that
our room was located in the corner of the building. I felt on my own for the first time and
loved it.

    I was not actually unsociable, but I really
didn't want to start making friends too quickly.
I had just broken ties with the friends back home
and was not anxious to burden myself with new
social obligations too soon. I did not like parties and so resisted the invitations of people
to join them for the big bashes. I just wanted
to be alone to do whatever I wanted and to enjoy
myself. I figured that there would be plenty of
time to make new friends once I was really set-
tled in.

    Then Mom got cancer.

    At first, I just told myself that everything
would be fine and I went on trying to enjoy my
new life. But gradually, over the course of the
semester, she got worse, and I began wishing I
hadn't chosen a school that was so far from home
because I had to depend on phone calls for news.
My family seemed to need me, and I couldn't be
there for them.

I also slowly began to realize that I needed them. I kept trying to recapture the great joy I had felt at my independence, but somehow all I was able to feel now was loneliness. I looked around at the thousands of faces on campus and realized that in my quest for solitude I had alienated everyone who had tried to be friendly. I now had no one to talk to about this horrible thing that was happening in my life.

I don't know why, after all my snubbing, Angela stopped by that evening just after I had had a long conversation with my dad about Mom's treatment, but she did. At first, I found it hard to talk to her at all, let alone open up about my personal problems. But she could sense something was wrong and after awhile I found myself confessing everything to her and finally crying while she hugged me.

It was Angela who first brought me to the sorority house. I hated sororities with their silly social functions, snobbish attitudes, and secrets. But I needed people now, and I was surprised to find how easily the women accepted me and made my pain their own. They really did become like sisters, and when my mom died, they grieved with me just like my family.

Now when I hear students talk about sororities and fraternities in the negative way that I did, I can understand their attitude and why they feel as they do. But when I remember my loneliness and despair and realize how much the sorority helped me, I am grateful for my sisters. And it's comforting to know that they are there for others, willing to help even someone whose mind is absolutely set on being independent.

Although this story is not likely to make any anti-Greek student participate in rush week, it may help that antagonistic reader see why someone would. The writer is trying to make her readers see that she was not one of those stereotypical women who waited impatiently for rush week and spent hours deciding on just the right wardrobe to impress the women at a particular house. In fact, she tries to break most of the stereotypes associated with "sorority girls" by emphasizing her desire for independence and her lack of interest in parties. She wants the reader to consider that there might be other reasons people join these clubs. In other words, by explaining her personal situation and her pain, she tries to break down some of the barriers between her and her antagonistic audience and to disarm her readers.

She also acknowledges the feelings of the opposition and even admits that she shared these same negative feelings with them. And she focuses on loneliness, a univeral emotion which has caused all of us, at some time or another, to act in ways we did not expect to act. She uses these emotions as common ground on which to build a new perspective on sororities. She hopes that by getting people to understand how it could happen to her, in this particular instance, she will get her readers to move away from their absolute stand against Greek life.

Persuasive writing is found in numerous forms: advertising, editorials, pamphlets on current issues, and a variety of newspaper columns such as those written by Mike Royko, Ellen Goodman, and George Will. Sometimes the persuasion is subtle and sophisticated, like Meg Greenfield's, and sometimes it is obvious, like that of most advertising campaigns. When we analyze the approach of these writers, we can see the attitude they expected their readers to have while they read.

Chapter 5

Being Evaluated

Sometimes persuasion takes a different form in which we are trying, not to "sell" an idea to someone, but essentially to sell ourselves or our knowledge. We are trying to convince someone that we deserve or know something, and we are evaluated on how well our writing proves this. In this situation, we can anticipate that our audience will listen in one of two ways, either as a critic or as a teacher.

The Critic

The critical audience is a judge. The critic reads the writing with an eye to what is wrong with it or evaluates the writer with an eye to accepting or rejecting the author as a person. This audience stance is very common and comes into play in a variety of situations: college entrance or placement essay exams, job or scholarship application letters, autobiographical sketches or personal statement essays that often accompany applications, and proposals requesting funding or support for a project.

The critic essentially is detached. The job of the critic is to evaluate and categorize the writings. In sifting through applications, for example, the critic will be trying to eliminate unqualified or lesser qualified applicants. The goal of a placement exam reader is to judge the paper quickly and evaluate it as something that either passes or fails. The critic's job, then, is to analyze and judge a piece of writing as either inferior or superior to others like it.

Let us evaluate three résumés from the point of view of the critic. These three women are applying for a high school teaching job in English. They are all qualified, having earned degrees from the same university. What distinguishes the résumés is the way each writer has highlighted her individual talents and unique experiences to make her résumé seem better than those of the other applicants.

Sample Résumés

DANA

DANA MILLER

Rural Route 2
Small Town, Illinois 60000
(123) 456-6789

CAREER OBJECTIVE: To obtain a position teaching high school English
in a community desiring
sensitive leadership
and quality education.

EDUCATION: Illinois State University
Normal, Illinois
B.S. English Education, 1986
Certification: grades 6-12
GPA: 3.4

PROFESSIONAL EXPERIENCE

March 9, 1986-Present STUDENT TEACHING
Normal High School, Normal, IL
Taught all four levels of English and a re-
medial reading class containing a majority
of students who are LD/BD. Responsible for
planning daily lessons, grading assignments
and tests, supervising and disciplining students, and completing administrative duties.
Assisted supervising teacher in extra duties
such as monitoring halls and detentions.

Interacted with administration and served
on the yearbook staff.

January 1985-September 1985
UNDERGRADUATE TEACHING ASSISTANT
Illinois State University, Normal, IL
Assisted in teaching two freshman English
composition classes. Taught writing lessons, graded papers, tutored students in
grammar, writing, and study skills, and
taught word processing. Developed an excellent rapport with students.

COACHING AND SPONSORING ABILITIES

Yearbook staff	Newspaper staff
Pom-pon	Drama club
Cheerleading	Speech team
Volleyball	Dance
Track	Computer club

PROFESSIONAL INTERESTS

Creative writing
British literature
Computers and writing

REFERENCES

Available upon request

Dana has several assets that are highlighted by this résumé.
Her career objective is clear and is phrased in such a way as
to compliment her future employer as someone concerned
with quality education. She has taken the time to describe
her professional and work experiences so that the nature of
these jobs is clear. Finally, she has highlighted how she can
be of service to the school beyond teaching by listing the
extracurricular activities she is able to handle. Since most
high schools are on limited budgets, being able to act as a
coach or sponsor is a real plus. Such activities also indicate
a willingness to work with students beyond the classroom;
few schools are interested in teachers who look on teaching
as an 8:00–3:00 job.

SARAH

Sarah Baron

Permanent Address   Current Address

    R.R. 2   167 Residence Hall
    Farm City, IL   Normal, IL ·

Personal Data

    Birthdate: June 9, 1964   Marital Status:
    Health: Excellent   Single
    Interests: Music,
    writing, sports

Education

    Illinois State University, Bachelor of Arts
    Degree, 1986
        Major: English Education with emphasis
               on writing and American
               Literature
        Minor: History
        GPA: 3.70 in major; 3.40 overall

Work Experience

    1983-1986   Undergraduate Teaching Assis-
                        tant, English Department at
                        Illinois State University.
                        Tutored in freshman English
                        intensive sections designed
                        for students with severe
                        writing problems. Worked in
                        University Writing Center with
                        students on a one-to-one basis.
    1982-1984   Writing Advisor, Simpson and
    Summers   Associates, public relations
                        firm. Supervised writing of
                        business letters.

Honors and Activities

    Honors Programs, Illinois State University;
    Dean's List (five semesters); Residence Hall
    Newspaper Committee (writer).

References

Placement Office   Simpson and Associates
Illinois State University   P.O. Box 87
Normal, IL   Adams, IL

University Writing Center
Illinois State University
Normal, IL

Although Sarah's qualifications may be as good as Dana's, she is not selling herself to the critic audience as effectively as Dana did. There is no stated career objective beyond the implied one that she wants the job for which she is applying. Her work experience is explained thoroughly, and she has listed her honors, but these qualifications are not going to place her ahead of Dana. She needs to sell herself by focusing on what she can do for the school. She has several useful skills listed on her résumé, but she has classified them as "interests." Each of these items needs to be translated into some kind of service; she might be able to coach some sports, to help with the music program, to sponsor the yearbook. But instead of using these as selling points as Dana did, she simply lists them as "personal data" as if they were not connected to the professional position she is seeking.

Also, Sarah's references are confusing. If she has a placement file on record, why are two of her references listed separately? Are these not in the file? If these are wanted, will the school have to make three separate contacts? This kind of confusion is not a good reflection on Sarah's ability to organize information. Finally, Sarah has not given any phone numbers for her residences. Although this may seem minor, it will be a major annoyance to an employer who wants to call her and cannot find her number. It may make Sarah seem less thorough, conscientious, and considerate than Dana.

JANE

Jane C. Wright

PRESENT
ADDRESS

1601 E. Washington
Normal, Illinois 61761
(309) 452-6666

EDUCATION

Illinois Community College
Assoc. of Arts--1972-74--Cum Laude

B.S. Secondary Education, Illinois
State University
Normal, Illinois 61761
May 1986
Major: English
Minor: Sociology

STUDENT
TEACHING
Mar.-
May 1987

Normal High School,
Normal, Illinois 61761
Taught Freshmen thru Seniors;
Literature and Composition

WORK
EXPERIENCE
Aug. 1979-
Present

I am a housewife and the mother
of four children

Aug. 1985

Jewel Food Store, Normal, Illinois
Cashier

Sept. 1976-
May 1978

Catholic Grade School, Monroe,
Illinois 62354
Full-time teacher: Predominantly
Grades 7 and 8

OTHER
ACTIVITIES

School committees
Church committees and projects
Charity projects

INTERESTS

Running
Some tennis competition
Reading
Music

Although this woman is the only one of the three with actual teaching experience, she is the least likely to appeal to the critic. She may be qualified, but she is not phrasing her qualifications in such a way as to benefit her. For example, because she has chosen reverse chronological order for her work experience, her teaching job is listed third, after her job as a cashier. Also, no one would deny that housewives work and perform valuable tasks that would greatly help a teacher, but just listing housewife and mother under her work experience does not capitalize on those skills. In the same way, the duties involved in her "other activities" could be explained to highlight the skills these duties developed and how they relate to teaching. Like Sarah, she could draw attention to her interests, especially competitive tennis, in such a way as to offer them as a service to the school. Finally, although the rest of the world may be ready to accept updated spellings for words such as "thru," it is not likely that a high school administrator will consider such an "enlightened" position an asset in an English teacher. Jane needs to follow strict conventional rules in spelling, punctuation, and grammar.

The critic, then, would quickly be able to evaluate these résumés, arrange them hierarchically, and eliminate two of them from the competition. Sarah's and Jane's résumés are simply not persuasive enough to pass the critic's test.

When we write for a critical audience, we need to be on our best behavior. We must make a good impression and beat the competition for the job, or the grant, or the scholarship, or at least be among those who are accepted. Care in every aspect of writing from overall planning to proper use of commas is essential.

The Teacher

It may seem to students that teachers are also critics, and in some cases, they probably are. However, usually the relationship between the writer and reader is different because the teacher feels responsible for the students' learning. It is the teacher's professional duty to help students acquire information and skills. When the educational system is working properly, the teacher supplies students with enough information and guidance so that they can perform the writing task well. The specific requirements for the task will be clear, and the student will be able to receive help with the task if needed.

Good teachers also read papers and tests hoping that the students will do well because that is a good reflection on them. They tend to be disappointed and self-critical when too many students fail. The critic usually has had no involvement in the learning or teaching process and therefore has no stake in the writer's success.

On the other hand, the teacher shares with the critic the judging stance, and the writer is, once again, in the position of needing to prove competence, this time in a particular subject matter. While the critic is looking to discover information about us and our qualifications, the teacher already has all the information about the subject matter that is needed and probably knows a good deal about us as well. The writer's job, then, is to prove to the teacher that the information and skills being tested have been thoroughly learned.

Also, rather than listening willingly, the way other audiences would, teachers may have to force themselves to read the thirtieth essay on the causes of the Civil War. And rather than assuming that what the writer says is honest and accurate, the teacher often reads assuming that the writer will make mistakes and may even be trying to get away with something. These factors all affect how much like a critic the teacher becomes.

The test and the academic paper are the two most common situations in which audiences assume the teacher stance. To help us imagine how this reader will respond to our writing, we can look at three students' responses to an essay exam on persuasion.

Sample Essay Exam Answers

Test Question: Explain the major types of support used in persuasive writing.

Answer 1

There are three major types of support used
in persuasive arguments: logical, psychological,
and emotional. Logical support comes in the form
of deductive reasoning (drawing a conclusion from
already stated premises) or inductive reasoning
(proving a claim by finding support for it). An
example of logical appeal would be the use of
statistics to support a general claim. Psychological support is everything a writer does to
prepare the reader for the message and make the
reader receptive to the message. An example of
this would be when a political candidate is sur-
rounded on stage by the flag, family members,
and a variety of important supporters. This
atmosphere creates positive feelings about the
speaker in the minds of the audience. The third
kind is emotional support in which the writer
appeals to the feelings of the audience, as when
patriotic feelings are aroused at a political
rally. Although logical appeals have been used
traditionally, modern research in persuasion has
emphasized the strong influence of psychological
and emotional appeals in changing audience
attitudes.

The above answer, from the point of view of a teacher, is
successful. It is efficient; the student has delineated three
types of persuasion. It proves knowledge; each of the three
types is explained and examples are provided. Although the
teacher may know other information that could have been
covered or other supporting details that could have been used
in addition to what is provided, the writer has displayed competence in the subject and the teacher audience would generally be satisfied.

Answer 2

For those of us who live in the 20th Century, persuasion is an everyday part of life,
especially in the form of advertising. In this
form, it has existed as long as anyone can
remember--all the way back to selling snake oil

in the Wild West. This is a long time for persuasion to be part of our country and that's why we
all know how it works.

Although ads use a variety of fallacies such
as begging the question and setting up a "straw
man," they are still very effective. One of the
reasons for this is that they use different types
of support. I would now like to discuss the major
kinds of support used in addressing an audience
persuasively.

The first type is logical. This type of support is based on reason and thus appeals to the
logical and rational side of the reader's mind.
The second is emotional which appeals to feelings
like fear, pride, etc. This means you try to get
the audience to agree with you by making them
pull out the old hankies. There are other types
of support that also work besides these. They
should be remembered, too, when writing, and they
will all come back to you because you see them
on TV everyday.

This is the kind of answer that tries teachers' souls. It
exemplifies what is usually called "B.S." The writer has some
basic knowledge (logical and emotional appeals), but this is
communicated in two brief sentences. The rest of this essay
is filler. The writer is trying to include any information that
can possibly be fit in: the kinds of fallacies, the nature of
advertising, the snake oil sales that were probably mentioned
in class. The writer is also just chatting with the audience
about how persuasion is a part of life, about how long advertising has been around, about the Wild West, and about how
we see examples of persuasion every day on television. None
of this proves knowledge, and the rambling is not likely to
make the teacher audience receptive to the two pieces of
information the essay does contain. This writer is filling up
space not only with extraneous information, but also with
extraneous words. At the end of paragraph 2 when the writer
does finally acknowledge that the topic is the kinds of support,
his first statement is that "logical support" is based on "reason,"

which therefore makes it appeal to the "logical and rational side" of the reader. The judging teacher should have no problem evaluating this answer.

Answer 3

        Emotional based on fear, pride, etc. Logical
    based on inductive and deductive reasoning. Psy-
    chological which makes the reader receptive like
    flags at a political rally.

        I think this question is unfair because it
    was not covered in the book or class.

This writer's approach to the teacher audience is also going to cause trouble. Since the stance of the teacher is one of authority and the job of the writer is to reinforce that authority by repeating the information learned, the criticism contained in that last sentence will not help the writer to succeed with this reader. The statement is not only impertinent, but also false. The writer of this answer has the same information as the writer of the first answer (logical, psychological, and emotional appeals), so the material obviously has been covered in class. The writer simply is not taking the time to prove this knowledge which is what the audience expects the student to do.

These three students clearly illustrate the best and worst ways to address the teacher audience. The first student recognized the authority of the teacher, proved that the information had been learned, and conveyed the information as efficiently as possible. The other two are insulting, discuss information without proving a command of the material, and waste the reader's time. Also, the purpose of these writings is informative, which makes the chatty attitude of the second response and the personal comment in the third inappropriate.

When our work is being evaluated, then, we need to be concerned about the impression we are making on the readers. We must be on our best behavior and make sure that our own attitude corresponds to what our readers expect.

Chapter 6

Sharing Information

Sometimes we write with the idea of sharing information that we have with others who want or need this knowledge. The situation is opposite to that of the teacher or critic in that we are now in the position of authority. We are also not personally involved in the information as we are when we are sharing ourselves. And our purpose is not to persuade readers to believe the information or to sell ourselves to a critic. Rather, we are simply trying to share our knowledge about a subject with people who are interested in it.

How we approach this task again depends on our relation to our readers and on the attitude they will have while reading. When we share information, our audience will probably be composed of either insiders or outsiders, people who know as much about the subject as we do or people who know very little.

The Insider

Certain groups share a common interest, situation, or knowledge base that makes them "insiders." We all belong or have belonged to at least one such group. Most of us, for example, have been part of a special social group at one time or another with whom we shared experiences and much inside information.

The most obvious characteristic of these groups is that they share a language, a way of talking about the world that is unique to them. Teenagers often have a list of adjectives for "good" and "bad" which changes so frequently that high school teachers have difficulty keeping up with the current slang. In the same way, professional groups such as lawyers, scientists, and educational administrators all have a specific vocabulary and manner of expression that they use with each other, with other "insiders."

The development of an insiders' language is partly a matter of convenience and partly necessity. As we learn more about a topic, our vocabulary for discussing this topic naturally increases. As we study a subject such as poetry, for example, we learn the specific terms that are used to analyze the genre. Thus, English majors move from a general knowledge of words, lines, and stanzas to specific terms such as "alliteration," "iambic pentameter," and "heroic couplet." The new language gives them the vocabulary they need to explain their analysis of a poem and to communicate more accurately that analysis to other experts.

But this language also keeps people out, excludes them from the insiders' group. Lawyers are perhaps most noted for deliberately developing a language that most people cannot understand. This ensures that people will need lawyers to explain and interpret legal documents for them. In most cases, people are happy to pay for the legal expertise, but objections have been raised when the document in question is one people feel they ought to be able to understand without the aid of a translator. This discontent has fostered "plain language" movements for documents such as apartment leases, mortgages, and wills.

Whether the motive is to promote better communication among experts or hamper the understanding of outsiders, insiders expect the language of their group to be used in any communication that is written for them. It would be very odd if students, for example, did *not* use their insiders' language to talk to each other about school matters. Therefore, even though the language may exclude others, among members of the group it is the natural and most efficient way to communicate.

The following paragraph was written by someone studying linguistics, an analysis of the nature and structure of language. Notice the use of insiders' jargon.

> Through linguistic surveys such as William Labov's study of the social stratification of a phonological variable throughout New York department stores, linguists are showing that there is a sharp increase in the percentage of use of a stigmatized variable in a working-class group, from the frequency of that variable found among members of the middle-class. Because of this sharp break, Labov and others are finding that in many cases, a speaker's social class can be approximated by studying the speaker's language. They are also finding that people are so aware of this break, whether consciously or not, that they align all speakers with similar dialects in related social classes. Thus, successful mimics of prestige dialects are considered to be upper class, while speakers using features of a low-prestige dialect are regarded as working-class, despite background, race, or intellectual capabilities.

To understand the above paragraph, the reader first needs a grasp of the vocabulary: social stratification, phonological variable, stigmatized variable, prestige dialect. The sentence structure is also written for an experienced, well-educated reader, thus identifying the subject matter of this insiders' group as not only specific, but also academic. In other words, the prose of this particular insiders' group is not meant for recreational reading!

When we write to fellow insiders, then, we must use the language of that group in order to prove our authority. We must also build on what is common knowledge for that group and not repeat information that we all already know. This audience is usually looking to a fellow expert for a little new information or at least a new perspective on a topic.

The Outsider

Writing for an outsider is quite different. This reader does not share our expertise. Sometimes this reader is ready and willing to learn from us, and other times our message is resisted. Sometimes there is a good deal of knowledge that separates the reader and writer, and sometimes there is very little. Each of these situations signals a slightly different reader stance.

The Outsider and the Expert

Sometimes experts need to explain their subjects to people who know very little about them, as when a doctor must explain an ailment to a patient without using medical terminology or when a nuclear physicist tries to explain radiation poisoning to the general public. Experts are valuable because they can specialize, and often nonspecialists need that expertise. In this situation, the experts must give up most of their exclusive language and talk to an audience interested in the topic, but not knowledgeable about it.

The above paragraph by the linguist revised for outsiders might read:

As soon as Eliza Doolittle, the cockney flower girl in *My Fair Lady*, began to speak, she was instantly identified as a member of the lower classes; her pronunciation gave her away. Thus for Professor Higgins to remake her into a member of high society, he had to work hard on changing the way she spoke—all those drills on the "rain in Spain" and "hurricanes hardly ever happen."

That pronunciation is related to class has long been evident. But in the past, researchers who tried to investigate this relationship got their data by asking people to read certain key words from a list. This method allowed for comparison between speakers, since each read the same list, but the speakers nearly always used a very careful, unnatural pronunciation. A recent study by William Labov, however, has shown that even features of casual, natural pronunciation are directly, systematically related to class.

The genius of Labov's method lies in his approach to getting natural pronunciation. Labov simply went into department stores, found out what department was on the fourth floor, and asked salespeople where that department was located. The question, "Could you tell me where women's shoes are?" regularly got the response, "Fourth floor"—giving Labov two examples of words with r. On the fourth floor itself, he simply asked, "What floor is this, please?" In each case, Labov then pretended he hadn't understood and thus got the salesperson to repeat the information with a more careful and distinct pronunciation.

To determine how pronunciation corresponded to social class, Labov compared sales clerks in three stores—Saks Fifth Avenue, Macy's, and Klein's. He reasoned that, because Saks catered to customers of a high social class, sales clerks at Saks would also be members of a higher social class than those at Macy's. He then analyzed all these pronunciations and found that the number of r's that were pronounced corresponded directly to the speaker's social class—the more r's, the higher the class.

The most noticeable difference between the two explanations of Labov is the word choice. In the second example, all the technical vocabulary has been eliminated. "Social stratification" becomes a "speaker's social class." The "phonological variable" becomes how New Yorkers "pronounced r's." The difference between high- and low-prestige dialects is explained as "the more r's, the higher the class." The same information is being communicated, but the range of people who can understand what is being said is much wider in the second piece.

Also notice the devices the author uses to help an outsider relate to the material. Eliza Doolittle and her language change are common knowledge. The social class distinctions are explained in terms of Saks, Macy's, and Klein's. The writer also gives examples of specific words and phrases to help us relate to the difference in the sound of the pronunciation. These devices take the subject matter out of the academic realm and make it something of interest to a more general reader.

When we write as experts for outsiders, we must keep in mind the expectations of the audience. Outsiders come to us expecting us to be honest. When they turn to a technical manual to help solve a mechanical problem, they expect the information to be correct. An outside audience also expects to understand what is being said. This may seem obvious, but one of the most common mistakes made by experts is talking over the audience's head or trying the audience's patience. When computers joined the ranks of general household appliances, the difficulty with some manuals was that they were not "user friendly." The explanations in them were too technical and complicated for the average consumer. Similarly, every student has felt that certain textbooks seem to be written not for those who need to learn the information but for those who already understand it and therefore do not need the book.

In other words, if we are experts writing to outsiders, we need to keep in mind how much our audience knows about the topic and adjust what we say to suit their needs. Our audience will become easily disgruntled if we fail to provide the information in a readable and easily accessible form.

The Outsider and the Reporter

A fire yesterday gutted a home at 13 West Street. The fire started in the basement of the home and rose quickly to the upper floors. The owners of the home were on vacation. Fire investigator Owens said that arson was suspected as the cause of the blaze because of the speed with which the fire spread.

Although there are many times when outsiders need to go to experts (doctors, lawyers, plumbers) for advice, people get most of their information about the world, not from the experts themselves, but from people who are specialists in relaying information. Newspapers, for example, do the information-gathering work for readers. Reporters inspect the news site, interview experts and other people involved, research background information, and condense all that they discover into brief articles. News magazines, research papers, encyclopedias, reference books, plot summaries, annotated bibliographies, abstracts, and annual reports are good examples of this kind of writing. Readers come to this writing looking for information as they did with the experts, but usually the stance they have is just slightly more skeptical. Readers recognize that newspapers and newsmagazines have biases, and before taking an encyclopedia at its word, they usually check its date of publication since knowledge in many areas increases faster than it can be printed. For example, any information on AIDS in an encyclopedia would be woefully inadequate.

Once again, then, when we write as reporters, readers will expect us to be honest in our recording of information, even though they may be more skeptical about its accuracy. They also trust us, as writers, to do all the necessary homework involved—to check out our sources before reporting what they said, to research background material, and to make sure the incident really did occur. It would be very embarrassing for the newspaper, for example, to find out that the house at 13 West Street was still standing.

The Outsider and the Voice of Experience

Another source of information is the voice of experience; people can learn from us when we have been through something and are willing to share the knowledge we have gained. Although readers often listen to this experience with great interest, they are more skeptical about it than about the advice from either the experts or the relayers of information. If we were to tell someone about an operation we had had, for example, our listener would be likely to remember that we had been unconscious through most of the ordeal.

On the other hand, there are many situations in which we feel someone could benefit from our experience. For example, the following paragraphs are part of a paper written by a senior student in math education. His audience was a group of math majors who had taken many math courses but who had not had any teaching experience. His goal was to make them reconsider basic mathematical principles from the point of view of their future students. As a student teacher, he had realized how much of his knowledge he had taken for granted, and wanted to share some of what he had learned with others.

> Think back to first grade when math was new to you. Numbers were meaningless at first, but you slowly acquired an understanding of them and started to successfully complete problems.

Whether you were aware of it or not, you had to learn a great many concepts before you could complete the simplest of problems. These concepts are so familiar to us that we actually need to stop and analyze them before we can teach them to someone else. When I first started to teach small children, I realized that I had forgotten how complicated the learning process is. I made many mistakes, and I'd like to keep you from making some of the same errors by getting you to think about one of those concepts we take for granted—addition.

Addition involves a series of complex steps in learning, and children must understand these concepts before they can solve an addition problem. Each step must be introduced separately and drilled until mastered. First, the concept of "number" must be understood, a stage in mathematics we call primary number work. Children in this stage learn the name, the numeral itself, and the idea of what a number represents. Visual aids and concrete materials are beneficial in this number work. Children learn through repetition that one button represents the number one and can be verbalized as "one."

This writer is not yet an expert either at math or at teaching. He is also not a specialist in relaying information. But he has something valuable to say, and his readers will be receptive as long as what he says and the advice he gives make sense to them. His goal is to make the readers see the information they have about math in a new way and therefore to add to their understanding of it. With their own knowledge of math, these readers could probably figure out how to teach the subject to children on their own. However, they are willing to listen so as to minimize their own workload by building on the information that he is willing to share.

It might be helpful to look at the three kinds of attitudes outside audiences might have toward our writing again. If we were writing about financial aid for college, for example, we could write as an expert if we worked in the financial aid office at the school and could answer specific questions about how to get money at this college. If we were reporting information on this subject, we might do research on the availability of money and write an article for the school newspaper. If we had applied for aid ourselves and been turned down, we could share this information with a friend who was trying to get aid.

Outsiders would expect to get the most specific and helpful information from the financial aid office and would trust this information the most. The newspaper article might inform the reader of the likelihood of students' getting financial help, but since the information would be general, the reader could not rely on this source too much. The information from the friend would have to be taken with a grain of salt, since the audience's financial situation might be completely different. We should perhaps also keep in mind that there are some readers who will doubt even the experts, who will feel that even with a doctor it is wise to get a second opinion. But the fact remains that that second opinion will most likely come from another doctor and not from just a friend.

As writers, then, we can expect our audience of outsiders to be the most skeptical if our only source of authority is our own experience. They will be less skeptical if we have done our homework, although they will still expect to see our sources and will expect us to rely on these more than on our own opinions. Finally, they will be most likely to believe us if we have proved ourselves experts in our field. Although it may seem that we are not likely to reach this stage until we have had considerable training and experience, many of us become knowledgeable enough in certain areas to be considered experts by certain readers when we are still quite young.

For example, as part of a unit focusing on audience, my students exchange letters with a group of seventh graders. These junior high students write to us first asking questions about college life. My students, especially the seniors, are certainly experts at providing the kind of information these seventh graders want to know. They are even more expert, for example, than the administrators or teachers who might have more years of experience at the school but who would not have the student perspective that the seventh graders want.

Depending on our subject, then, we may easily find ourselves in all of these situations, adjusting what we know to suit the needs of each of these audience attitudes.

PART THREE

Audience and the Writing Process

In the first two parts of the book, we have discussed the relation of audience to the writer, the subject, and the purpose, as well as how audience influences style. We have also discussed how important it is to imagine the audience and to anticipate this audience's reaction to what we say. To be effective, writers need to envision their readers, so as to anticipate their needs and to meet their expectations.

This envisioning is an inherent part of the writing process itself. A clear sense of audience helps the writer with every part of the composing process, from the initial planning stages to final proofreading. To see how audience analysis is an integral part of composing, we need to examine the influence of audience on each stage of the writing process.

Chapter 7

The Stages of the Writing Process

For the purpose of convenience, the writing process will be discussed in terms of five stages. However, writing is dynamic and does not always proceed in a logical manner. We each have our own stages that we go through to produce a piece of writing, and we may not follow exactly the stages indicated here. We each must work out the best way to proceed, and these stages are only meant as a broad indication of how the process often works.

Stage 1: The Assignment

"Oh, Jim, I still haven't written that invitation to the Meyers!"

The writing process begins when we are given a reason to write in the form of some stimulus or assignment. Usually, we are given the assignment by someone else (a boss, teacher, committee), but sometimes we set a goal for ourselves (write an invitation to the Meyers, for example). Either way, there is suddenly some task set before us that we need to respond to in writing. So, the first job is to analyze what it is we need to do.

Purpose and Audience: Questions to Consider

What is the purpose of the assignment? What does the assignment ask us to do?

Are we trying to share something of ourselves, a story about our past or an opinion that we hold?

Are we trying to persuade people, to change their minds, to influence them, to argue with them, to sell something to them?

Are we trying to pass along information that we have, to advise people, to report to them?

Are we trying to accomplish more than one of these aims? Are we trying to sell ourselves, for example, in which case we must both share personal information and be persuasive? Are we passing along information in the hope that people will be persuaded by that information to better their lives in some way?

Subject Matter and Audience: Questions to Consider

What information needs to be communicated to this audience?

Is this audience well informed on the topic and are we therefore providing details or a new perspective? Or is the audience unfamiliar with the information and are we giving them the basics?

Is the audience only interested in the subject matter without caring particularly about who is doing the writing? Or are people only interested in what is being said because we are the ones saying it? Are they perhaps interested both in what we say and in who we are?

What is the audience's stance on the topic?

Are the audience members neutral, antagonistic, receptive, or apathetic?

Style and Audience: Questions to Consider

To whom is this writing addressed?

If we are writing to ourselves or to a friend, have we made our
writing personal and informal?

Is the audience familiar, and can the individuals in the audience
be identified? If this audience is large, can we generalize
about audience needs based on the individuals in the group
whom we do know? Have we adjusted our style to suit the
size of the group and its relation to us?

If the writing is addressed to a composite audience, what generali-
zations can be made about the group? What kind of composite
portrait of the group can we develop? Consider such things
as age, status in society, background, education, and level of
authority.

Stage 2: Getting Started

Do Meyer invitation TODAY — Find out what the heck is in
Springfield.

After we analyze exactly what the assignment is asking us
to do, to whom it is to be addressed, and what kind of subject
matter and style are appropriate for these readers, it is time
to start getting ideas down on paper. There are several good
techniques for this such as brainstorming, during which we
list everything we can think of to say on the topic, and free
writing, in which we "just start" composing on the topic to
discover what we have to say and how much we know. Sometimes this process begins with just a single idea (what's in
Springfield), and sometimes it helps us decide on most of
the ideas that will be found in the final copy.

Any device we use to help us get ideas down on paper can
be greatly aided by considering the audience. For example,
if we are writing about the current developments in a particular situation at work to a group of co-workers, we might begin
by making a list of everything that has happened in just the
last few days or since the last report the workers received.

On the other hand, if some of the workers are new and are not familiar with the background of the situation, the brainstorming may need to include a list of events that will put the concern in perspective for the newcomers. Keeping our audience in mind, then, will help us to better define the scope of our topic during this preliminary, information-gathering stage.

Stage 3: The First Draft

Dear Mr. and Mrs. Meyer,
    My Aunt Joyce told me that you two would be coming to Illinois during the month of . . .

Dear Dan and Deb,
    My name is Laurie and I'm the niece of Joyce . . .

Hi!
    You don't know me, but . . .

The first draft is where our brainstorming or preliminary thinking begins to take shape into something that could be identified as a paper. Sometimes, these first drafts go well, and we produce something that lays a good foundation for further drafts or, because of one of those rare inspirational moments, is actually very close to final copy. Sometimes while composing the draft, we discover what we want to say, and the draft becomes part of the getting-started stage. And other times, we discover that we have not done enough pre-liminary thinking, and we get a false start (or several, as in the example above). The draft then leads us back to the beginning of the process, to reviewing the assignment and the audience once again.

When first drafts go well, we usually get from them a good sense of whether we are accomplishing our purpose, and record in them the basic information we need to include if we are to achieve that purpose. Once again, a sense of audi-ence can help us here. If our purpose is to persuade, for example, keeping in mind the audience's attitude about the subject will help us judge our effectiveness. Are we saying things that will make a hostile audience simply stop reading? Are we wasting time by trying to convince someone who is already on our side? How informed is this audience on our topic? How much background do these people need? What we want to accomplish, then, is closely linked with what we want from our readers and what they expect from us.

Stage 4: Later Drafts

Dear Mr. and Mrs. Meyer,

I suppose I should begin this letter by introducing myself. I'm Laurie, the niece of Joyce Galat. My Aunt Joyce wrote to me last week and told me that you would be coming to Illinois during the month of January and that you might enjoy a visit to Springfield.

I just wanted to let you know that I would be happy to pick you up in Peoria and take you to Springfield for the day. We could visit X, Y, and Z and have lunch at _____.

If this trip ~~would be of interest to you~~ interests you/if you think you might enjoy this/if this would be fun—something—call me when you get into town.

Next letter: to Aunt Joyce—warning her never to do this to me again!

The number of drafts a writer produces between first and final copy depends on the writer and the difficulty of the task. Most of us must make several attempts before the paper is "finished," and even then we know we could still revise. Also, drafting is seldom a linear process; we do not produce one whole draft and then go back and revise the whole paper into draft 2. Instead, we often begin our revision process immediately and change words, sentences, and paragraphs as we compose. Thus, as the above letter of invitation shows, some parts of the draft will be in final form while others are still in the developing stage.

However, after we have something down on paper, the drafts which follow usually help us refine our ideas and style.

We can focus more on the details of the piece. We check the information we have included to see if something is missing or if something can be cut. We, perhaps, outline the paper to make sure it is organized. We check on our purpose to make sure the paper really is accomplishing our goal. We make sure the style is consistent, that we were not formal and distant in one paragraph and chatty in another.

Again, these concerns are a natural part of composing and do not occur at any one time. But a piece of writing cannot be analyzed and revised until we actually have something down on paper. We can, therefore, think about revising as coming *after* the initial attempt to compose. Revising is also, of course, related to audience. We have already noted that the amount and kind of information we need to include depend on what the audience already knows. In the same way, the type of voice we choose depends on our relation to our readers, and the most effective organization depends on what these readers need to hear first and what we want our last impression on them to be.

Stage 5: The Final Draft

Dear Mr. and Mrs. Meyer,

I suppose I should begin this letter by introducing myself. I'm Laurie, the niece of Joyce Galat. My Aunt Joyce wrote to me last week and told me that you would be coming to Illinois during the month of January and that you hoped to visit Springfield.

I just wanted to let you know that I would be happy to accompany you on this trip. I could pick you up in Peoria, where I understand you will be staying with friends, and we could make a day of it. There are several historic sites to see and I know some wonderful restaurants for lunch.

If you still feel this trip would interest you, please call me when you get into town and we can arrange a day.

I look forward to hearing from you soon.

Sincerely,
Laurie

In a final draft, we usually focus on "repairs." The paper has been constructed; we now need to go over it one more time to make sure no detail was forgotten. It is a time to check for errors in spelling and punctuation, to check the format and layout, to make sure that each sentence is properly constructed, and to be sure that our words precisely convey our meaning.

However, even the judgments we make for final copy depend on our audience. It may seem that proofreading would be the same for any piece of writing and that we would always identify and correct errors, but this is not the case. When we write for ourselves or for close friends, we may do little if any proofreading. We may be completely unconcerned with how the piece "looks" and may be very careless about sentence construction. On the other hand, if we are writing for an error-counting English teacher, we may sweat over each comma and every capital letter.

In other words, whenever we make a choice about what to do, whether we are choosing something as small as a word or as large and encompassing as a purpose, we decide what is "right" or appropriate based on the needs of the reader. When we ask ourselves if our style is formal enough, we also have to ask, formal enough for whom? When we wonder if our organization is effective, we must ask, effective for whom?

Good writing, appropriate voice, effective organization, achievement of purpose, and correct style are not absolute or objective terms. They do not exist in a vacuum but in the dynamic arena of human interaction and communication. Without considering audience, without recognizing that there is someone, some real person, who will actually take the time to read what we write and to try to understand it, no real communication is possible. In other words, without a reader, even if that reader is only ourselves, there is no point in writing and there are no clear guidelines for what effective writing is.

Chapter 8

Illustrating the Stages of the Writing Process

In order to see how audience enters into each stage of the writing process, we can follow a writer, Cherie, as she tries to contruct a paper. We will follow the production of the paper and Cherie's thoughts on audience from her first draft to her final copy.

Cherie is a student in an advanced composition class. The assignment is to write a persuasive paper about a subject she has a direct interest in—and that is the challenge of the assignment. To be persuasive, she must be able to consider the other side. At the same time, she must select a subject she has a genuine personal stake in, and that commitment will tend to make it difficult to sympathize with the opposition. We can see Cherie struggle with this challenge throughout the process.

Stage 1: The Assignment

This was her assignment:

> Your topic for this assignment will need to be something controversial, something that has more than one side to it. There is a catch, however. You must select a topic that you are personally involved with or have some real stake in. You must select

an issue that you care about and that you've had some real-life experience with.

In your paper, you are to present your side in a persuasive way, using your own experience and outside sources to support your point of view.

Cherie chose the topic of voluntarily childless couples because she and her husband belonged to this group. She wanted to try to explain to people why some married couples might decide not to have children.

Audience

Cherie's primary audience is couples who are in the midst of making a decision about whether to have children—fence sitters. She hopes to help them see the benefits of choosing against parenting. As Cherie explained it, her essay "may not be persuasive to those who want children, but to those couples who are undecided it may be very persuasive." A secondary audience is people who cannot understand why a married couple would choose to remain childless (parents of childless couples, for example). She wants to get them to understand that there are benefits to the life-style as well as to see that not all women make wonderful mothers. Finally, although Cherie does not intend to speak to the antagonists, she is aware of them, and simply hopes not to offend them too much. She also realizes that her essay might act as something of a pep rally for childless couples who perhaps are feeling pressured to change their minds; she lets them know they are not alone in their decision.

Purpose

The primary purpose of Cherie's essay is *persuasive*. She needs to sell her idea to her readers and to try to convince them to see her side. Since she is dealing with fence sitters, she needs to draw their attention to all the arguments that might push them to her side. For those readers who are simply trying to understand why anyone would make this choice, she needs to establish the validity of her position.

Subject Matter

The focus of the writing is on the benefits of remaining childless. Cherie is drawing on personal experience, on interviews with other childless couples, and on readings to support her views.

Style

Cherie is writing to a composite audience. She is drawing on what she knows about the people who are struggling with this decision as well as on thoughts of couples who regret having children. She knows that some of them have heard arguments against having children, but she also knows that some of her readers simply will never have considered having children as optional. Her audience, then, will have a range of knowledge and information. Her main concern is to keep her voice from sounding defensive and angry and to establish her credibility through the quality of her argument and her writing. She acknowledged that "this voice [was] difficult to achieve and maintain throughout the essay."

Stage 2: Getting Started

Cherie's first task was to gather all the information she needed and to sort through her own feelings on the topic. She began her writing with a brainstorming list of her thoughts.

Brainstorming List

Main Point:	Children are not for everyone.
Establish Credibility:	I've been through this. Women should be able to pursue their careers or other interests without restrictions.

Involve Audience: All adults crave time entirely for themselves. Parents complain they don't have this time. Childless couples enjoy this time without feeling guilty about the children.

Problem: Society feels childless couples are selfish, deprive themselves of enrichment, lead unfulfilling lives, and women are incomplete without motherhood.

My View: Not everyone wants children. Not everyone is very good at parenting. This should be a personal decision.

Support: Parents, nonparents, newspaper, magazine article.

Conclusion: Life can be equally satisfying with or without children.
Take pride in your personal accomplishments; this is not dependent on kids.
Birthrate is dropping--that's good.

Analysis

Cherie's brainstorming list is more complete than many such lists turn out to be. But Cherie had thought about this issue a long time and had fought this battle against the stigma of remaining childless many times. She knew she would have a good deal to say and felt that her anger might make the paper get out of control. So she wanted to establish early (1) what she wanted to say (that children are not for everyone), (2) her own right to tackle this topic (her credibility), (3) that there is a problem because of society's expectations, (4) that the decision should be a private one and not society's, (5) where she would get her support, and (6) what conclusions she would draw. She knew that the very thing that gave her a serious interest in this topic was what could also make her lose her objectivity. As I said earlier, this was the challenge inherent in the assignment, and Cherie struggled with it all through her drafts.

Stage 3: First Draft

Cherie's first draft is an example of expressive writing being used to discover her motivation for choosing this topic. It is also a way for her to get rid of some of her emotions about the topic so she can approach it more objectively. It is a strong statement about why this topic is so meaningful to her.

Draft

When I was born thirty-five years ago, my mother didn't give it a second thought. It was understood that the reason you got married was to have children. And the sooner, the better. If a woman didn't become pregnant soon after marriage, something was presumed to be wrong and other women felt sorry for her and at the same time, superior. After all, they were more complete as women--they had given birth to a child.

Today, the child birthrate in the United States is dropping dramatically, and I have helped to contribute to this phenomenon. I don't want to have any children. It's been my choice for a long time. At the age of thirteen, my mother gave birth to twins, followed immediately thereafter by a nervous breakdown. While my mother was recovering, I became a "mini" mom, assisting my grandmothers and aunts with the babies. It was not fun. I loved my little sisters dearly, but the restrictions they placed on my early teen years can never be replaced. I decided I did not want to spend the best part of my life looking after others.

```
    The decision not to have children will be
one that I'll never regret. I am adult enough to
recognize that not everyone was cut out to be a
parent. I am not.
```

Analysis

Most of this draft just disappears as the paper progresses since Cherie's ultimate purpose is not just to explain her personal reasons for not having children, but to talk about this topic as a social issue. But she is coming to grips with the reasons behind her decision and the reasons behind her anger at the society that will not let her make this decision without arguing with her about it. The rest of her composing process, then, can move beyond her "I am not" statement to arguments and explanations that will be relevant to others. She does lay a foundation for certain ideas that will show up in later drafts, such as society's view of childless women as incomplete, the restrictions of children, and the question of choice.

Stage 4: Later Drafts

Cherie's next draft fleshes out many of the ideas in her brainstorming list. But she still is struggling with audience. Much of her second draft is still expressive—aimed only at self and a very sympathetic audience—and not persuasive for fence sitters. At this stage Cherie not only wrote her drafts but also commented on the process. These comments are included because of what they reveal about the importance of audience in her composing process.

Draft

```
     Children = Little babies. Dirty diapers.
Crying. Whining. Unwanted responsibility.
Restrictions. Stress. Pressure. Strain on
relationships.
```

Whenever someone asks me, "How many children do you have?" the images listed above flash through my mind. I immediately get defensive and reply, "None--by choice."

I try to explain my feelings. I don't dislike children. My niece and nephew are the most precious children in the world to me. It's just that I have known since childhood that having children was not for me. My girlfriends played with baby dolls--I played with trucks and blocks. My kindergarten teacher wrote a very concerned note to my mother because I played with the masculine toys instead of with the grocery store carts or dollhouses. This was a very serious matter in 1957. After all, the theory was that all little girls grew up to be mothers and housewives.

I am called selfish, but the fact is I simply made a decision. I am part of the first generation to have this choice. In the past this was not an option. Women usually became pregnant immediately after becoming married because it was the proper thing to do. Consequently, many women had children without thinking very much about it and certainly before they were really ready for the responsibility. Some turned out not to be very good at being mothers, but this too was something they could not admit. A recent article in the Pantagraph entitled "Motherhood Report Separates Myth from Reality" reported that in a survey of 1100 women between the ages of eighteen and eighty, only one out of four mothers had a predominantly positive experience with motherhood. But the myth persists, and I feel it every time someone asks, "How many children do you have?" never anticipating what my answer will be.

I do not have children for a simple reason-- I do not want them and my husband does not want them. We discussed having children before we got married and came to this mutual decision to remain childless. We feel it has made our marriage stronger, and the Pantagraph study agrees: the

majority of women questioned said that "most aspects of their marital relationship had suffered
with the advent of children." Many couples without children seem to have more satisfying re-
lationships with their spouses than those who
have children. This may be because the stress
and pressures of the children are not there. The
couples with children tell us, "You'll be sorry
when you're older." But when I reply, "What about
now? Doesn't our happiness now count?" they don't
have a reply.

My husband and I also both realized that we
were not meant to be parents. We personally feel
all couples should discuss their parenting abilities before marriage, but unfortunately, many of
our friends did not. From our viewpoint, we see
the child as the one who suffers.

There seems to be a trend today toward
couples postponing parenthood, or deciding
against it entirely. This has happened in both
my family and my husband's family. And many of
my co-workers and friends, who are now in their
mid-thirties, with successful careers, have decided that they like their life-style without
children.

As more and more couples make a conscious
decision to either have children or not have
them, I feel that our society will eventually
accept the fact that not all couples are parent
material. _Time_ magazine refers to working couples
without children as "DINKs," meaning "double in-
come--no kids." I am happy to be called a "DINK."
At last it appears that our life-style is finally
being recognized and accepted--at least by the
media.

Writer's Comments

After a conference with my writing teacher, I went back to
the office and discussed the paper with my co-workers. They
read the first two pages of my draft and laughed. "You're writing

this to your mother-in-law," was their comment. The realization finally came to me. I thought about my teacher's comments about the anger in the paper and knew my colleagues were right—the paper *was* being written to my mother-in-law. When I rewrite, I will do it with my own mother in mind because she understands my decision.

I see my real audience as undecided couples who are unsure about having children. I also wanted to keep from offending those who do not share in my views. But the subject matter tends to offend some people. There are people who do not think the subject needs to be discussed. Women should marry and have children—end of discussion. My purpose is to try to achieve neutrality and say that women should have children, but not all women. It should only be those who truly want them.

But the subject matter is also one which I have strong feelings about. My wish is that people wouldn't badger me about my decision. I still feel it is a personal decision and no one else's business. I hope that my rewrite is better and that I successfully channel out my anger.

I arranged the paper with all the negatives about children in the first paragraph. I felt this would catch the reader's attention. But I feel the need to rearrange so as to portray this as a major social issue and not just a personal one.

Analysis

At this stage, Cherie has written a fairly effective personal opinion essay. She clearly reveals and explains her opinion about having children and supports it with examples from her own experience. She has explained the social pressures that couples feel to have children and outlined the reasons that couples choose to say no to these pressures. She is also beginning to find a way to make this issue more public—by pointing out that she is not alone in her decision. In fact, there are so many couples like her and her husband that the media have come up with a new name for them. This outside support will help her in her next draft both in making her argument less personal and more socially relevant and in proving that she has done her homework as a reporter.

Stage 5: Final Draft

In her final draft, Cherie has moved away from her personal story to the issue itself. This does not mean her personal knowledge and commitment are no longer important; they still form the basis for her point of view and her authority on the subject. However, she has become one of many women struggling with this issue and a spokeswoman for them. Once again I have included her (this time amusing) comments about the writing process.

Draft

In the October 12, 1987, issue of Time magazine, the cover story asked the question, "Are Women Fed Up?" Joyce Maynard, an author and mother of three who writes a weekly syndicated column, said, "If women are unhappier, it is partly because they are trying to pull off something that can't be pulled off, except on Thursday nights in 'The Cosby Show.' Women have been told they can have--even ought to have--husband, children, and career, all perfectly managed. It is a lie." The article went on to say that women seem to be realizing that this is a lie and are choosing not to try to have it all. One obvious choice for some women is not to have children.

Careers are one big reason many women are choosing this option. Many women have found themselves perfectly content to continue their climb up the corporate ladder. For these women to have a child at this stage in their lives would be a tremendous career setback--a setback many are not willing to accept. These women have found their lives fulfilled with their careers and do not have the desire (or time) to have children. Caroline is an excellent example. She and her husband, who is also an executive, are frequently on the road for business trips. Caroline has progressed rapidly at her company and feels she may progress even further, if she can maintain her

present performance level. For Caroline to have
a child at this point in her career would be dis-
astrous. She feels personally satisfied with her
career choice and has decided with her husband
not to have children. She is unwilling to sacrifice her hard-earned career for a child, and
her husband is not willing to sacrifice his
career either.

Many career women also feel that the equal-
ity of their marriage will suffer with children
because women are usually the primary caretakers
of children. They immediately find themselves
juggling full-time career and full-time motherhood with little help from their husbands. The
October 16, 1987 edition of the Pantagraph reported the findings of a survey of 1100 women
between the ages of eighteen and eighty. The survey found that "one out of five married women
thought their husbands gave them so little support, they might as well not be there at all."
The article went on to say that "50 percent did
not think much of their husbands as fathers and
described them as uninvolved and overly critical." This kind of inequality in the workload at
home can lead career women to think twice before
becoming mothers.

Other couples feel their marriages are
stronger because they do not have children. These
couples have more time to devote to each other
and to pursue shared hobbies. One of the reasons
Cherie and Mike chose to marry was their mutual
decision to have no children. If either of them
had felt differently, they do not feel their marriage would have the qualities they now enjoy--
limitless privacy; plenty of time to pursue their
careers, hobbies, and social activities; and time
left over to spend alone with each other. They
do not believe they could have been a partner in
a marriage with children. This honesty is what
attracted them to each other, and is one of the
qualities that makes their marriage strong. Again
the women in the Pantagraph poll agreed: The
majority believed that "most aspects of their

marital relationship had suffered with the advent of children" since children's needs often must come first.

In its title, "Motherhood Report Separates Myth from Reality," the article also indicates another reason why women may choose to remain childless. As one woman explained it, she imagined that she would be like Beaver Cleaver's mother, "all nice and neat and happy and sweet-- vacuuming in heels and pearls and baking cookies for the children." However, "after the babies arrive, daydreams go from happy cookie bakers in heels and pearls to more desperate, beleaguered thoughts." In their survey, they determined that only one out of four mothers had a predominantly positive experience with motherhood. The survey indicated there was "a lot of ambivalence in between." Statistics like these make women much more skeptical about motherhood than they have ever been.

The strain of motherhood can be seen in women of the previous generation, such as Clara. Her career was raising four daughters. Her husband's career took precedence over hers as he was the breadwinner and provided the family with the basic necessities of life. His viewpoint of motherhood was that the mother took care of the children, all housework, cooking, and other associated "women's work." It was not his place to offer any help, since he had worked all day. When Clara was recently asked if she would do it all over again, her answer was not surprising: "No, I wouldn't." She went on to say that while she loves her daughters dearly, she has been taking care of them for the last thirty-six years, and she is tired of it. Motherhood stopped being fun many years ago.

But for Clara there was no real choice. In the past, not having children was not a real option for most women. They usually became pregnant immediately after becoming married because it was the "proper" thing to do. Consequently, many women had children without thinking very much

about it and certainly before they were really
ready for the responsibility. Some turned out
not to be very good at being mothers, but this,
too, was something they could not admit.

While children do give their parents many
rewarding personal experiences, childless couples
can't help but see the dark side of parenthood--
exhaustion, fatigue, responsibility. The plea-
sures that children may give don't surpass the
stresses they may cause. Thus, the couple decides
not to have children.

Perhaps the most valuable outcome of this
new opportunity for choice is that mothers who
have babies will genuinely want them. Every
woman, just by nature of her sex, will not feel
obligated to take on this responsibility. The
children will be cared for by mothers who made a
conscious choice to be mothers, while those who
chose not to become mothers can pursue other interests. Many women have already realized that
they were not meant to have children. Perhaps
the ideal situation--that of choice--will be
achieved in the near future, and women will become happier with their chosen roles.

Writer's Comments

The style I used in this essay was more formal, and I tried to
make a logical, objective argument that not all women are meant
to become mothers. In rewriting the paper, I felt I did achieve
more objectivity. But it was not easy!

While rewriting the paper on Thursday evening, I was inter-
rupted by the doorbell. It was almost 9:00 and my husband
wasn't home, so I did not answer the door. I kept hearing these
kids outside, and when I looked out the front window near the
door, I found them teepeeing our trees out front. I was furious.
There went all my objectivity for that night!

I guess my biggest problem with this paper is that I can't
understand why couples choose to have children. I must be
blinded by all the negatives. But I tried to put myself in a
mother's position and see her viewpoint. I hope this paper is
more impartial.

The essay was arranged with a current headline from *Time* in the opening paragraph. This was done to illustrate to the audience that this is a major social issue, one which many women are facing today. I proceeded then to answer the question, "Why?" I used examples of women I know, and I used an article from the newspaper. I think these help my credibility. It was sad for me to realize that I don't know any happily married women with children. I was going to use their commentary in my paper to make it more balanced. But in looking at co-workers, I was still unable to interview a happy mother. So this section of the paper is not as strong as I hoped it would be.

Analysis

Cherie's final paper is a good persuasive essay. In the process of composing she has used many of the techniques we have discussed in previous chapters.

First, she has identified her audience. She has chosen to go beyond herself (draft 1) and beyond the nodders (draft 2) to include the fence sitters and to take into account the antagonists.

Second, she has examined her subject matter and recognized its inflammatory quality. She has therefore decided not to start with the list of negatives and her defensive reply, but with a *Time* magazine cover story.

Third, she has a clear purpose which is defined *in terms of audience*: to try to persuade fence sitters to make a wise decision while not antagonizing her opponents too much.

Fourth, because her audience is a composite one, and because, by her own admission, she could not find "a happy mother" to balance her own negative personal experiences, she has tried to become more objective by removing herself from the piece. When she does refer to herself, it is in the third person. The subject is no longer presented as her personal story. This decision makes the writing more formal than previous drafts.

Fifth, in terms of dealing with the fence sitter she has involved the audience through images such as Beaver Cleaver's mother, through examples of real couples who have chosen this option and are happy about it, and through appealing to the universal desire for quality child care.

Sixth, since Cherie decided against basing this paper on the voice of experience (since she could find no voices for the opposition), she has moved into the role of reporter. As a reporter she has done her homework. Cherie has included sources to back up her opinions.

Notice how each of these techniques is affected by audience. Her initial decision about audience determines everything else she does, as her own comments show.

Why Bother?

Writing is difficult, and experienced writers tell us that even practice does not make it easy. There seem to be so many things to worry about: content, organization, sentence structure, word choice, grammar. Audience may seem like an additional, unnecessary burden!

But the fact is that a good sense of audience makes all of the other writing tasks easier because it gives us a purpose and focus for our writing decisions. It forces us to remember that writing is communication and not just a meaningless, time-consuming exercise. It makes us think about the people who will read our writing and makes us try to reach them rather than to just fill up pages. It makes us anticipate how what we write will be received, and that makes us better critics of our own writing. And it forces us to imagine our readers' needs and thus helps us to decide what information to include, how to organize it, how to approach the topic in an interesting way, and even how much we need to worry about mechanics.

In other words, audience makes writing meaningful. It makes writing a genuine attempt to communicate something we know or feel to someone else. And it is because communication is the only reason we have language and use it that audience *must* matter whenever we write.

Index